YOUR
FUTURE
LIVES

YOUR FUTURE LIVES

BY

KELYNDA
EDWARD SPARKS
BRAD STEIGER
ENID HOFFMAN
NICKI SCULLY
MARY DEVLIN

Whitford Press

1469 Morstein Road
West Chester, Pennsylvania 19380 USA

International Standard Book Number: 0-914918-82-6
Library of Congress Catalog Card Number: 87-63415

Edited by Skye Alexander and Lynn Kendall
Published by Whitford Press
A division of Schiffer Publishing, Ltd.
1469 Morstein Road
West Chester, Pennsylvania 19380

Manufactured in the United States of America
This book may be purchased from the publisher.
Please include $2.00 postage
Try your bookstore first.

Contents

1 The Eternal Quest

by Kelynda

The Present is the point at which time touches eternity. Of the present moment, and of it only, humans have an experience analogous to the experience which God has of reality as a whole; in it alone freedom and actuality are offered them.

C.S. Lewis, The Screwtape Letters

Discovering the Pattern of Your Destiny

Whether you believe in reincarnation, in Heaven, or in no afterlife at all, one fact is evident: the only time you have to live (and prepare for your afterlife) is now. You may have been reincarnated a thousand times—as every famous person from Cleopatra to King George III—but you cannot relive those lives. Nor can you wait until your next life to deal with an issue or fulfill your destiny; how do you know you will have a chance?

Because the past is unchangeable and the future uncertain, the present is crucial. If this life is all you have, every choice you make may decide your destiny; the present moment suddenly becomes holy and irreplaceable.

This chapter will not tell you about past lives.[1] It will, instead, teach you some ways to find the patterns and meanings of your present life—this one, the one that seems alternately dull and frightening, with occasional flashes of pure joy. There are three tasks you must perform in this lifetime: finding and fulfilling your destiny, dealing with karma, and learning to live well. I offer questions, not answers; questions you must ask yourself. You have a destiny, a mission: what is it? There are interlocking levels of life: how can you live deeply and intensely on all of them? I offer techniques—using crystals, music, visualization, game-playing, journal-writing, and meditation—for finding your destiny, dealing with obstacles, and getting to know the parts of yourself that have been suppressed, repressed, oppressed, and forgotten. There are quotations from great minds, and (for the eager, the curious, or the scholarly) a bibliography with suggested readings.

As you read, remember that I too am working all these things out for myself; I have not (by any stretch of the imagination) solved all my problems, dealt with all my fears and scars, and learned to live on the highest plane. I'm still struggling; writing this was part of my struggle. As I write, I pray for you, my readers; I pray that my words will help you find enlightenment, not be a stumbling-block to you. As you work through the exercises and ponder my ideas, pray for me as well.

For convenience, I consider and deal with life issues on three levels: the physical level, the psychological level (including how to work with the Shadow), and the spiritual level. Do not confuse these artificial divisions with anything real; they are simply a convenience. Each level or aspect of life influences the others; you cannot change one without changing the others.

The three levels are not like a layer cake, with the spiritual frosting on top. Think instead of clear acetate overlays, each of them a map of different colors and patterns. When the three are stacked, you can look through them to see the overall pattern of your attitudes. This three-layer film is the screen you see the world through; only the rarest of us ever see the world with total clarity.[2]

On every level, this chapter deals with two essential concepts: that there is meaning and purpose in your life, a meaning and purpose that are at least partially discoverable and that you should try to discover; and that good and evil exist. If you choose to explore the "pleasures" of evil in this lifetime, you will pay. There are consequences to your acts and attitudes; what you do matters.

What if I'm wrong, and there is no afterlife at all? Then the way of life I've outlined here still will have given you satisfaction, meaning, and joy. You will have discovered richness and beauty in ordinary things, and you will have helped other people.

Some Special Terms

I use the term *karma* in a special way. Leaving aside the question of the contribution of previous lives, I define karma as the specific set of situations and problems that you're in this life to deal with. If your destiny is to help abused children, your karma will probably place you in some painful situations in order to sensitize you to the effects of abuse.

Destiny, like karma, has a special meaning in this chapter. It is not a fatalistic, predetermined doom that you cannot avert. Indeed, you alone choose whether you will fulfill your destiny. It is your purpose in life, the mission you were created for— and it isn't always glamorous.

Your destiny is not a station on a single-track railroad, a place you must reach if you go forward at all. It is the center of a labyrinth, a labyrinth that (once you can safely look back from the center) is constructed on a principle: the principle of whatever lessons you needed to learn to be able to perform the task in the center of the maze. The design is, in fact, karma.[3]

The maze image has one drawback: it may reinforce the common misconception that if you have a mission, you have one single mission, to and for which you should sacrifice everything else. Nothing should stand in the way of your destiny—not friends, family, rose gardens, music, anything. But that attitude is destructive and wrong. Your destiny is not the single issue on which you'll be judged. And you have many missions, some of greater importance, all at the same time. As you grow older, you'll finish some early ones and start new ones. You are not a machine, designed to fulfill one function and then be discarded.

What Should I Do?
The Question of Destiny

The process of finding your destiny starts by looking at the raw materials of the self: Who are you? What do you like, love, hate, fear? What do you want to spend your time doing? What have you already struggled with? What are you good at doing?

You were not chosen by lot to perform your destiny; you were created to fulfill it. *Fulfill* has two shades of meaning, as different as the implications of *finish* and *complete*. Fulfill—in its sense of finishing—means to achieve, to reach your goal. This view considers only the purpose or end, not the means. That's a black-and-white, pass-fail, binary view. Failure or success is judged solely by results. This is the ordinary way of looking at success.

But *fulfill* has another meaning, one closely linked to *fulfillment* (a sense of satisfaction, of having found a place and a task for oneself). In its sense of completion, fulfill means to carry out a mission, satisfy a requirement, serve a purpose.

You embody your destiny; in completing your task, you make yourself whole. This view considers your life as a gestalt: the process and structure of all you do, the texture of your daily life, the integration of your destiny with your ordinary obligations to other people, with your pleasures, with the way you think. Your destiny is more than a trophy brought back from a cosmic scavenger hunt: how you try to get it is actually more important than whether, in fact, you succeed. The means justify the end.

Conventional marks of success—large houses and cars, your name in the headlines, fan letters from strangers—are irrelevant to fulfilling your destiny. You can easily fulfill your destiny and not become rich and famous. In fact, that's the pattern most people follow. Others become famous only after they are dead. Vincent Van Gogh, for example, whose paintings now sell for tens of millions of dollars, sold only one painting while he was alive. A few people get rich for other, incidental reasons; only a tiny percentage (impossible to determine) actually win fame and fortune to fulfill their destiny. It doesn't matter either way; success is not the point. Fulfillment is. As Albert Einstein said, "Try not to become a man of success, but a man of value." That goes for women, too!

Your destiny is unique to you, because it is more than a single set task that you must perform. It is a complex puzzle—a maze—that includes personal relationships, self-healing, accomplishments at work, spiritual attitudes, and a thousand other factors. The invisible effect you have on others is just as important as the achievements you're aware of and proud of. Your destiny is a process of developing your soul; if you turn willfully aside from it, what are you doing but crippling a soul?

Spiritual development goes on whether you're aware of it or not, in ordinary tasks as well as in meditation and prayer. This chapter is designed to help you become aware of yourself so you can discover where and how to go in order to create a whole self, live a complete life, and thus fulfill your destiny.

Work and Destiny

Your job is not necessarily your destiny, although it can be a part of it. The right job can help create the complete life. And the process of coming to know yourself, which will help you understand your destiny, can help you understand what kind of job is best for you. The same techniques can be used to help you make other choices: where to live, ways to change, and so on.

To help you understand your relationships—with lovers, family, friends, co-workers—you can do the exercises with someone else. More details will be given in the section on interpreting the results.

A Few Notes on Technique

I offer six basic techniques in this chapter, and all the exercises make use of these techniques—crystal-choosing, visualizing, journal-writing, art/music exercises, meditation, and game-playing. The techniques appeal to different powers and parts of the brain. Though one technique may seem to work best for you, I urge you to try all the techniques (though you don't have to do all the exercises); you owe it to yourself to develop your hidden skills. However, don't try them all at once! Do a few now, one or two a day for several weeks, skip a few days, then do some more. You'll overload yourself and quit if you try to do too much at once.

Before you begin any of the exercises, you should relax. Physical comfort helps; so does a relaxation ritual (such as preparing and drinking herbal tea, doing yoga stretches, or whatever suits you best). Deep-breathing exercises are also useful. Breathe in on a count of nine, feeling the clean air fill you, and breathe out on a count of nine, feeling impurities and tensions slip away. After seven such breaths, you should be ready.

After doing the exercises, you may want to record your findings. You'll also need a notebook for the journal exercises. If you choose a notebook, keep it only for your exercises; also, you should use a pen or pencil that's comfortable in the hand and encourages easy writing. You may feel more comfortable typing your journal entries. If (like me) you've been spoiled by a computer, use that. If typing is too cold for you, or computers make you nervous, stick with a notebook. If you feel limited by the slowness of writing longhand, use technology. Keep all of your papers together and private. Date what you write (it's convenient for future reference) and list what question you're answering, if any.

The crystal-choosing exercises are based on the list of stones for *The Crystal Tree*.[4] You don't need to have the book to do these, but you do need a range of stones: colored and clear, opaque and crystalline. If you don't have the proper balance of stones, you can't trust the results. Why? Because in order to choose, the options must be available for you; if you limit your options, you limit the effectiveness of your choice.

To choose crystals, lay the stones in a shallow dish (wood is nice but not necessary) or place them in a cloth bag large enough for your hand. Close your eyes and let your fingers and hands choose. They will sense the vibrations.

The visualizing exercises stretch your imagination. They help you test your choices before you have committed yourself to them. They also help you remember things you have forgotten or repressed. To do them most effectively, lie back in a comfortable chair, on the grass or earth, or in a warm bath. You can also do these floating on your back in a pond, but make sure someone is with you and that the water is safe!

Journal exercises use both the right (intuitive) and left (verbal and analytical) sides of the brain. You are not writing for your English teacher here (not that I want to insult these underpaid and under appreciated heroes). Do not worry about grammar, syntax, spelling, or the outline form. Write what you feel and think; you'll find that ideas come when you're not forcing them. Unless you're already comfortable with the process of writing, it's best to take a few minutes to think about the exercises before you get out your notebook. When you have several ideas, uncap your pen and open to a clean page (or boot your word-processing program). During the time you are doing these exercises, you should also record all your dreams in the notebook. They will offer additional insights into your patterns.

Art and music exercises help you explore your feelings and tastes. All the arts—music, dance, painting, sculpture, drama, poetry, literature—help us express feelings that we otherwise might not be able to reach and sense. You may watch a Western movie because it makes you experience certain feelings: the sense of freedom and wilderness, the battle of good and evil. It helps you test yourself: What would you do in the hero's situation? How does anyone get to be a bad guy in a black hat? Would you have given up everything to cross the plains in a covered wagon? It's also comfortable because the good guys always win. Through the exercises given here, you can discover some of your hidden emotions, sometimes by doing art—drawing or singing or dancing your feelings—and sometimes by experiencing art—listening to music that helps you feel.

Meditation and prayer are so familiar that they don't seem to be exercises. In these areas, I make tentative suggestions; you must establish your own relationship with the Inner Light, and no prayer exercise will help unless you are willing to listen as well as speak.

Game-playing can be done alone or with others. The game is Smoke, a metaphor game.[5] Played for yourself, Smoke consists of a list of metaphors for the self. ("If I were an animal, I'd be a lioness; if I were a mythic creature, I'd be a dragon; if I were a body of water, I'd be a waterfall; if I were a tree, I'd be an oak.") In the complex likeness and interweavings of metaphor, a sense of the self emerges: not the self as expressed in conventional ways, but the true inner self, rarely expressed. But you have to be honest. ("Though I think it's more respectable to be a well, I know I am a waterfall.") In the difference between the reality and the wish, I learn about the assumptions I was raised with: that I (as a daughter) was expected to be hidden, motionless, silent, and available, not open, exuberant, rapid, noisy, and a little dangerous.

You have to choose your metaphors honestly and not judge yourself by others' standards. If you're a flowering cherry, don't feel bitter or guilty because you're not a hickory. The point of the exercise—of all the exercises—is self-knowledge and self-acceptance.

Table 1: Crystals and Their Meanings

Rose Quartz

Physical: Friendship, intimacy, closeness.
Psychological: Harmony and affection; close family ties; the need for love and approval.
Spiritual: Surrender to God.
Shadow: Giving in, lack of self-assertion, going along with the crowd.

Red Cullet

Physical: Individualism, passion, and sexuality.
Psychological: Passion, creation, art. Independence and rebellion.
Spiritual: Spiritual transformation and renewal, the spirit of seeking.
Shadow: Jealousy, self-centeredness.

Jasper

Physical: Restlessness, change, curiosity.
Psychological: Spirit of seeking, self-examination, analysis.
Spiritual: The spirit of the quest, of the pilgrim.
Shadow: Change for its own sake—or the refusal to change and grow.

Carnelian

Physical: Warm and affectionate friendships, parties, and celebrations.
Psychological: Emotional ties based on knowledge of the other person, not on mystery and uncertainty. The need to understand and analyze relationships.
Spiritual: Reverence for life. The attitude that pleasure is of God and is therefore holy. Mystical union with God and all creation.
Shadow: Manipulativeness, lack of self-respect, over-indulgence, hiding behind a social group.

Cat's-Eye

Physical: Insight, shewdness, vision.
Psychological: The gift of understanding others' problems. Often the mark of someone who is dedicated to helping others.
Spiritual: Willingness to forgive, understanding the flaws of yourself and others.
Shadow: Judgmental spirit, cattiness, gossip.

Brown Agate

Physical: Caution and good judgment. Slow and careful preparation.

Psychological: Self-discipline.

Spiritual: Penance, justice, scrupulous fairness.

Shadow: Pessimism, gloom, worry, often over petty matters. Insecurity and fear.

Green Quartz

Physical: Strength of character, self-esteem.

Psychological: Blending the unconscious with the conscious. Willingness to face your own dark side. The ability to interpret dreams.

Spiritual: The Kingdom of God within you.

Shadow: Nightmares, phobias, emotional problems. The separation of spiritual and physical life.

Aventurine

Physical: Great physical enjoyment, health, taking pleasure in the body.

Psychological: Balance between body, soul, and spirit. A healthy and innocent enjoyment of physical pleasures.

Spiritual: Freely offering of the body to God.

Shadow: Physical illness, stress, and separation from (or too much absorption in) the body.

Hematite

Physical: Enduring love, desire controlled by idealism, complete commitment.

Psychological: The discipline to transform dreams into reality. Sustained commitment to a dream.

Spiritual: Continuing devotion to God despite adverse circumstances.

Shadow: Rigidity, fault-finding. Inability to make a commitment or stick to a project.

Sodalite

Physical: Achievement, success, hard work rewarded.

Psychological: Getting your just deserts—knowing what you deserve and asking for it.

Spiritual: Freedom from greed, taking no thought for the morrow.

Shadow: Materialism, greed, lack of compassion.

Chevron Amethyst

Physical: Organization, structure, neatness.

Psychological: The final integration of the personality.

Spiritual: The order of heaven.

Shadow: Snobbishness, wrong priorities, inhuman bureaucracy.

Amethyst

Physical: Psychic talents combined with common sense. Great success.

Psychological: Psychic powers used well, self knowledge and self-control.

Spiritual: A true spirit. Proper values.

Shadow: Using psychic knowledge for destructive purposes (very dangerous).

Crystal (clear)

Physical: Psychic abilities and clarity of outlook. Emotional harmony and peace.

Psychological: The integrated personality. Good relationships with others based on self-respect.

Spiritual: Clear views of spiritual truth.

Shadow: Arrogance, fear of change.

Crystal (half-clear)

Physical: Confusion, hasty or prejudiced thinking. Not letting yourself see the whole situation.

Psychological: Hiding the truth from yourself (usually to protect someone else).

Spiritual: The beginning of wisdom: knowing that you don't know.

Shadow: Refusing to trust yourself.

Silent Stone (white)

Physical: New beginnings and ideas.

Psychological: Waiting for the right time to make new beginnings.

Spiritual: The start of a new way of thinking. Protecting new ideas from hostile people.

Shadow: Overcaution or overeagerness.

Montana Agate

Physical: Memories and persons from the past turn up. Opportunities to correct past mistakes.

Psychological: Unconscious worries or influences from the past.

Spiritual: Remembering past problems in order to avoid them in the future.

Shadow: Restraint, fear, lack of forgiveness of yourself and others.

Smoky Quartz

Physical: The ability or need to conceal yourself from other people. A dramatic temperament.

Psychological: Hiding your true self in order to be liked or accepted. Adaptability.

Spiritual: Struggling to find a true path. The faith is there, but the way is not evident.

Shadow: Self-blame, over sensitiveness.

Onyx

Physical: Strength, courage, endurance.

Psychological: Getting to the root of the problem—a painful but necessary process.

Spiritual: Rebirth after a period of suffering and dryness.

Shadow: Giving up; refusing to enjoy anything for fear it will be taken away.

Determining Your Destiny: Exercises

1. What are you like?

These exercises are the basics of self-knowledge. You may feel foolish telling yourself what you like and dislike, but how often do you really consult your own tastes and wishes? It's far more likely that you do what's convenient, expected, or fashionable. Answer honestly; concealing the truth cheats only yourself. These exercises can be repeated annually to reflect your growth and change.

Crystal Exercise: Choose three stones from a group of stones and crystals. The first represents your personality, the second your motivations, the third your way of self-expression. For interpretations, see Table 1.

Visualizing: Imagine yourself doing something you enjoy. Is it active or quiet? Are you alone or with others? If you're with others, are you competing or working together?

Journal Exercise: Write a dialogue with yourself. Write as though you were writing to a new pen pal; ask yourself what you like, want, enjoy. If you like something and are afraid of it—whether it's sex, rock music, psychic work, or whatever—write a dialogue between the part that enjoys the forbidden and the part that fears it.

Music Exercise: Discover what your five favorite pieces of music are. These will change over time, so you should think carefully about what you like best now. Listen to them all—not necessarily in one session—and think about why you like them and how they make you feel.

Smoke: Play Smoke with yourself. Some categories you might use are:

tree	piece of clothing
weather	sense (sight, hearing, etc.)
kind of architecture	bird
period of history	animal (mammal)

animal (reptile)
fish
mythic creature
book
machine
geometric shape
artwork
stone
plant
flower
insect
light (sunlight, electric
   light, etc.)
breeze or wind
metal

tool
ornament
texture
smell
landscape
body of water
planet
character in a book, play,
   or movie
music
food
drink
language
skill

2. What Are Your Best Choices?

These exercises help you find the best choices for your life. The crystal exercise indicates the nature of your talents; the others help you find which directions may be best for you. By imagining yourself in other situations, you learn which choices are wrong before you invest your time and energy in them. For those who want specific career counseling, there are professional tests to measure levels of skill, talent, or creativity; these are listed in the bibliography.

Crystal Exercise: Choose three stones from a group of stones and crystals. The first represents your chief talent, the second your creativity, the third your way of expressing yourself. For interpretations, see Table 1.

Visualizing: Imagine what daily life is like in different fields or professions that you're interested in. Be honest and think logically. If you're thinking of being a reporter, for example, don't just think of interviewing celebrities and getting a byline; think of tight deadlines, writing about events that may upset you, and having to read the newspaper every day.

Journal Exercise: Think back to three important choices in your life. Write a story about what would have happened if you had chosen differently in each case. How would you be different? Would you be happier or less happy? If you feel you made the wrong choice, think about ways to change the consequences of your choice. What have you learned from the choices you made?

3. What Are the Patterns of Your Life?

These exercises are designed to help you discover the meaning in the apparently random events of your life. In order to do so, you must first remember the events and feelings— remember them honestly and think about their meanings. Then you must look for the patterns, using both analytical and metaphorical thinking. The process itself may be painful; if you have had a very difficult life, you may want to go through these exercises with a counselor.

Crystal Exercises: Choose three stones from a group of stones and crystals. The first represents your early life, the second your current life, the third your possibilities for later life. For interpretations, see Table 1.

Visualizing: Remember the three best times in your life. What made them so good? Could you recapture that feeling and use it in other ways? Remember the three worst times. Why were they so bad? Could you have done anything to improve them? What did you learn from them?

Journal Exercise: Write your autobiography, focusing on the one area of life that has given you the most trouble (relationships, possessions, family, whatever). You may want to try this using several different viewpoints.

Art Exercise: Draw, paint, model, or otherwise express how you felt at the best and worst times of your life.

Metaphor Game: Come up with as many metaphors for the pattern of your life as you can: for example, your life might be a spider-web, a train station, a thundery August afternoon, an unfinished painting, an adventure movie, and a lost cat wandering through strange forests.

4. What Stands in Your Way?

Walls, blocks, obstacles: these exercises are designed to identify and help you clear some of the psychological, emotional, and spiritual barriers to growth and change.

Crystal Exercise: Choose three stones from a group of stones and crystals. The first represents your chief stumbling block, the second an unconscious block, the third a block involving family or relationships. For interpretations, see Table 1.

Visualizing: Imagine your frustrations, blocks, and problems as a wall. What shape and color is it? Who built it? What is it made of? Are there gates? Talk to it and listen to it talk back. Whose voice does it have?

Journal Exercise: List what stands in your way; think of twenty ways to get around it, through it, or over it. Don't censor your list; just write as fast as possible. Even if something seems to be nonsense, write it down.

Art Exercise: Draw, paint, model, or otherwise express all that prevents you from doing what you want to, and then express ways to conquer those blocks.

Metaphor Game: Come up with as many metaphors for the obstacles in your way as you can. For example, they might be a wall, a lid on a box (with you inside), a long wait in line, a flat tire, a lion in your way. Then match ways of dealing with the obstacle to each metaphor: you might climb the wall or build a staircase to the top, saw a hole in the lid and climb out, read or meditate while you wait in line, fix the flat tire or hitchhike, and make a friend of the lion.

5. *What Does the Shadow Know?*

"Who knows what evil lurks in the heart of man? The Shadow knows!" That old radio-serial tagline summarizes the next set of exercises. The Shadow is not evil; it is the hidden, unaccepted, unloved side of the self, and it knows things you have been told to forget.

> The Shadow stands on the threshold between the conscious and the unconscious mind, and we meet it in our dreams.... It is all we don't want to, can't admit into our conscious self, all the qualities and tendencies within us that have been repressed, denied, or not used.[7]

Only by examining the Shadow can we understand our own potential for cruelty and creativity, for hunger and rage and shame as well as for kindness. Once we have accepted our own Shadows, we can learn to love our neighbors, forgiving them for their trespasses against us, because we admit that we also trespass. We can also love ourselves, finding it possible to forgive our own sins—and to believe in God's forgiveness—because we have forgiven others.

These exercises will begin to put you in touch with the hidden side of yourself—one of the most important steps in the process of enlightenment.

Crystal Exercise: Choose three stones from a group of stones and crystals. The first represents the nature of your Shadow, the second your way of repressing it, the third your way of overcoming it. For interpretations, see Table 1.

Visualizing: Imagine your Shadow. Is it a male or female, your own sex or the opposite? Does it look like anyone you know? Talk with it: What does it want? Whose voice does it have? What does it do for a living?

Journal Exercise: Continue your dialogue with the Shadow. Write an entry from its point of view (perhaps one of the other exercises, perhaps a new one).

Music Exercise: Listen to forbidden music. Dance!
Smoke: Play Smoke with your Shadow.

6. *Is This Worthy of an Immortal Being?*

If you suddenly realized that you were immortal, you would begin to see that the choices you make now will be reflected not just for a day or a year but for eternity. You would start asking yourself if what you were doing with your life is worthy of an immortal soul. You would change your life to reflect that new vision of yourself, the white flame noble in you, lasting forever, created by a loving God for a specific purpose, and answerable for the way it expressed itself in life.

That urgency, freshness, and passion are the way we are supposed to live. Your choice of work, your relationships with other people, your willingness to learn and grow and change and forgive, your attitude toward the created Universe and toward the Creator—all are transformed by the realization that what you do matters, every second matters. Certain questions become urgent: how do your choices look, not in the light of the next day or week or lifetime, but in the light of eternity? Are you, *now,* living in a way that befits an immortal? Because you are an immortal soul. What you do matters. Stop dreaming of your years as a gold prospector or a harem slave in the seraglio of Topkapi. The years that matter are the ones passing now; they are the only ones you can change.

These exercises are designed to help you see yourself in the clear light of eternity.

Visualizing: Imagine your destiny—and your ordinary life—in the light of spiritual values. What is the holy thing to do? Imagine yourself explaining your destiny to God.

Journal Exercise: Write about the responsibilities of an immortal being. Why is being a soul, which will never die, different than being soulless? Do you feel different about yourself when you think of eternity?

Meditation: Pray or meditate about your destiny. Ask for guidance.

7. Will This Draw Me Closer to the Spirit?

These exercises, like the ones in the preceding section, are not only useful in the annual summing-up of self but in daily life. They can help you make essential judgments and decisions; the last meditation should be repeated daily or more often.

Visualizing: Visualize the kind of spirit life you want to lead. How will your choices affect it? Think of all the consequences.

Journal Exercise: How do you see God?

Meditation: Pray or meditate about your spiritual life. Express your thanks, worship, and ask questions. Take time to listen quietly for answers as well.

Interpreting The Results

Interpretation is an intuitive process. You should prepare for it, as you've prepared for all the exercises, with relaxation techniques and rituals. You should also wait a week after completing the last of the exercises before you try to interpret. The process of interpretation is the same for both the destiny and karma exercises; you may want to spend time interpreting each set, and then slate a weekend for pulling it all together.

Ideally, you should interpret the results while alone on a weekend retreat, somewhere quiet and away from home. At least take the phone off the hook and arrange to be alone at home.

If you are in a serious relationship—perhaps considering marriage or a lifetime commitment—you may want your partner to do these exercises as well. Then the weekend interpretive retreat can be done together. Sharing your feelings, metaphors, exercises, visions, and artworks can be the basis for a fruitful discussion of how your lives will mesh and how they will be held separate. If you don't feel you can trust your partner with these innermost feelings, it's time to re-examine the relationship.

The first step is to read everything you've written. It may hurt. Rereading some of the memories, daydreams, and ambitions will cause you the same pain as rereading the old diaries or love letters you wrote that rainy spring ten years ago. As you read, jot down recurring themes and desires.

If, over and over again, the results of your exercises tell you that you are warm and social, that you have an eye for beauty, that you need to see immediate results, that praise and approval are important to you, you know that solitary and dry jobs are not for you. You'll never be happy as a long-distance truckdriver or an economist. If you like trucks or economics nonetheless, you could be a dispatcher or mechanic or a teacher of economics. In any case, the stones (taking into consideration your other aptitudes) give the clearest idea of what fields are best.

Here's an example of the process.[8] Rosemary came to me with a problem: she knew she wanted to grow and change, but she couldn't decide what job would best express herself. She had already made many of the other discoveries in finding her destiny: she had married a loving husband (having discovered that heterosexual marriage and family life were for her), she had found the proper place to live, she had decided that she wanted children. All that remained undetermined was her career. After going through some of these exercises with her, I discovered the following pattern:

—She liked people.

—She had a great deal of patience.

—People had always come to her for advice.

—She had some medical training and was interested in health issues.

—She had an analytical mind.

—She was detached. She knew her own boundaries and did not over identify with others.

—She had a strong urge to help others.

Combining practical, intellectual, and emotional factors, I advised her to get involved with counselling. But which kind? The crystal she had chosen was adventurine: a combination of body and soul. She would do best as a yoga instructor and counsellor or as a massage therapist. She felt the latter best fit her needs and is now studying acupuncture.

But work is not the only part of your destiny or the most important. Being yourself is. Gradually you'll begin to see patterns in the wishes, the metaphors, the music even, patterns that express you. Then it's easy to see the ways that your personality can be expressed in your life—ways of molding your life to the pattern of your soul.

Angela came to me for a reading, which revealed that she was unhappy in her job and her life generally. However, the problem with work was only a symptom of a deeper lack of fulfillment in her life. She was strongly psychic and knew she should have been using her powers to help others; instead she was terrified by them and tried desperately to repress them. As a child, she had been punished for knowing too much, and she deeply feared further punishment. Yet repressing her psychic energies was a drain on her vitality, and the powers, since they were not consciously accepted or controlled, worked their way into her dreams and frightened her further.

Instead of repressing her abilities, she needed training in how to use them. Through six months of hard work, she cleared the original block, learned to harness her abilities, and began to change her life. Now she is an established, skillful, and compassionate psychic reader. She doesn't have nightmares. She has a sense of fulfillment, knowing she is achieving her destiny through using her innate talents. And she has a more satisfying job as well—a change that came about naturally, because of the change in her.

Angela's story illustrates the truth that unused abilities

come back to haunt you. Through the above exercises, you have discovered much more of who and what you are. You should know as well what you want. But what of the obstacles in the way? What about karma?

Dealing With Karma

Traditionally, two kinds of karma affect your life. *Pralabd* karma, the kind you're born with, shapes your current life and is traditionally considered to be the residue of previous lives. *Kriyamen* karma is the kind you create in this life, which will shape your future life.[9] For the purposes of this chapter, pralabd karma is simply called karma.

Pitfalls of Karma

The concept of karma is liable to a very serious abuse, one that many deeply spiritual people avoid, but one that I have frequently encountered. Not everyone who defends this abusive attitude understands all the motivations and problems inherent in it; they are laid bare here.

The traditional view of karma blames misfortunes—from birth defects to business failures—on the sins of previous lives. It was also used in India as a method of social control: because everyone was born into the caste he or she "deserved," it was easy to believe that the lower castes, including the Untouchables, were exploited and outcast only because they were spiritually inferior.[10]

Even nowadays, some hold the opinion that the Ethiopians are starving because they are reincarnated Nazis suffering for having destroyed the Jews. But what karmic debt did the Jews and Gypsies and Poles and Lithuanians incur, that they had to die so horribly in the ovens of Dachau and Auschwitz? And why—if the victims were being punished for a karmic debt—

did the Nazis have to suffer for killing them? They were only carrying out the law; no executioner is prosecuted for murder when he pulls the switch on the electric chair.

That attitude is a symptom of the worn-out blame-the-victim mentality: she was asking to be raped, walking alone at night; she must have provoked him to hit her; if you were good, your parents wouldn't abuse and neglect you; her husband drove her to drink; if they'd behave, we wouldn't have to lynch them; if they had been civilized, we wouldn't have taken their land. They're poor, Black, women, starving, oppressed, raped, abused, conquered in this lifetime because they were naughty in a previous life.

It's comforting to think that way for two reasons: you don't have to do anything to help them (whatever them it may be) because they brought it on themselves and they have to work out their karmic debt. It excuses you from helping other individuals, and it excuses you from trying to eradicate war, poverty, prejudice, and child abuse by changing society, since the victims of these horrors brought it on themselves. Anyway, it's spiritual to suffer, and you wouldn't want to interfere with their destiny.

The second reason is that the privileged, white, or wealthy person no longer needs to feel kinship with the miserable—no longer needs to wonder if those awful things couldn't happen to him or her. They brought it on themselves; I must be spiritually superior, because I haven't had those things happen. Worse, the natural guilt-fed hatred the upperclass feels towards the underclass is reinforced by wondering what the latter did in their previous lives to deserve it. It's a splendid opportunity to despise the victims while self-righteously condemning them.

The victim who believes this has a worse time yet: it's already too easy to think any disaster is your own fault. Margaret, like most abused children, had believed that she had deserved the abuse; she made excuses for her abusive parents. Years of therapy helped her find emotional health by showing her that it was not, after all, her fault. Only after she was able to recognize that the problem had been not in her, but in her violent and unloving parents—to feel and accept her own rage at the abusers—could she forgive them. Imagine her feelings when she was told by the half-baked that it had been her own fault after all.

Not everyone who believes in traditional karmic reincarnation falls into this trap, and even those who do are usually unaware of the self-righteousness it causes. But it is a very serious problem. Is it really enlightened and spiritual to equate the social stratification of power and success with spiritual holiness—or is it a recycled version of the divine right of kings and the presidency above the law?

If you do believe in reincarnation, you can avoid the trap by keeping in mind that the next turn of the wheel may find you begging on the streets of Calcutta. If you don't believe in reincarnation, you can look on karma as I do: not as a punishment for past sins, but a preparation for future achievements. Christ's healing of a blind man addresses this problem directly. The disciples asked, "Who sinned, this man or his parents, that he should be born blind?" Jesus replied, "It was neither that this man sinned, nor his parents; but it was in order that the works of God might be displayed in him."[11]

Our karma—painful or easy—is not for punishment or reward, but to help us perform the works of God. Dealing with karma is not, therefore, accepting your fate because you're being punished; it's part of the pattern of your life.

To return to Margaret, she came to me feeling furiously angry and also unspiritual. What if it had been true? What if she had been punished for something awful in a previous life? "The worst thing was the helplessness. I couldn't stop it. Now I'm told that I deserved it. If it's true, I'm going to start hating myself again. What can I do?"

Over weeks of work with me, Margaret began to understand the abuse not merely as a horrible and meaningless event that had scarred her permanently—an event she likened to being hit by a train. She became aware of the role that the abuse had played in shaping her life. It was an important part of her pattern, though not something she had deserved. She began to see that since she could never be rid of all the effects of abuse, she should use what she could of the experience. At my request, she listed what she had learned from the experience. Here is her list.

—I'm a survivor. If I could go through that, I can go through anything.

—I think I'm more compassionate than I might have been. I can help and understand those who have suffered, and I'm even beginning to understand what drives the abusers. They've been hurt, too.

—I have learned about forgiving other people. That makes it easier to forgive myself, too!

—It helped me choose my job. [Margaret works to publicize the plight of the abused.]

—It made me depend on God. I know what I believe and I've tested it. If all that couldn't shake my faith, nothing can.

—The effects of abuse drove me to therapy and to other ways to try to understand myself. I've been forced to learn a lot about myself that I might not otherwise have known.

Viewing karma as a preparation for future achievements, rather than as a punishment for past sins, seems to be a much more constructive attitude. It helped Margaret reconcile the sense of purpose and design her spiritual commitment gave her with the truths she had learned in psychotherapy. It can help those with much less severe problems as well.

Hans Christian Andersen said, "Every man's life is a fairytale written by God's fingers." In certain myths and fairy tales, the happy ending is only reached after the proper question is asked. The proper question about karma is not "What did I do to deserve this?" but "What am I supposed to learn from this?" When you stop worrying about being punished for past lives and begin to see karma as a kind of training, you can start to fulfill your destiny in this life—and thus improve the future life.

The following exercises are similar to the exercises for getting to know yourself and for determining your destiny. But these exercises are designed to help you understand how the circumstances of your life work into the pattern—the pattern you've already begun to perceive. In order to see your karma clearly, you must be absolutely honest. That's painful; you may be able to do it only in stages. Just tell the truth as you see it when you're working; later it may be changed by remembering or understanding other incidents or factors. If you have had a particularly difficult life, or if you find yourself getting depressed, you may want to talk about some of these issues with a trained, professional therapist.

Dealing With Karma: Exercises

1. Are You Resolving It or Repeating It?

Certain situations come up over and over again in our lives. Psychologists know this as the repetition of a trauma; to a metaphysician, it also has karmic significance. If you don't resolve the central conflict, you must repeat it. These exercises will help you identify some of the recurring themes in your life.

Crystal Exercise: Choose three stones from a group of stones and crystals. The first represents the nature of your karma, the second your hidden feelings about it, the third the training it is giving you. For interpretations, see Table 1.

Visualizing: Visualize yourself stuck in a situation that has endlessly repeated itself in your life—conflict with a parent or in-law, a dead-end relationship, a self-destructive act, whatever. Imagine yourself resolving it instead of repeating it.

Journal Exercise: Write about a repetitive situation. When was the first time it happened? Does it remind you of anything in your family history? How do you get past the block when it occurs? What's the benefit to not resolving it? Why are you afraid to let it go?

Art Exercise: Draw (or otherwise express) your central conflict. What does it look like?

2. Can You Forgive?

Forgiveness is necessary but difficult. Edith Cavell, about to be executed by the Germans for smuggling refugees out of the country, said, "I must have no anger or bitterness toward anyone." Holding onto rage and pain, instead of forgiving, is crippling. Yet forgiving isn't easy; it entails acknowledging that you have been hurt (and are therefore vulnerable) as well as accepting that you too can hurt people (a hard admission to make, and part of dealing with the Shadow). It also entails understanding another's motivations.

All the understanding, all the compassion in the world, will not help unless you seize your own power and let go of the pain. Until you forgive those who have hurt you, you're still in their power. Your feelings are still controlled by their actions.

These exercises are designed to help you work through some of the pain and anger of your hurts, and then to help you forgive.

Visualizing: Imagine yourself forgiving your worst enemy and asking forgiveness from someone you've harmed. Then do it!

Journal Exercise: What can't you forgive? Why?

Music Exercise: Listen to healing music. Repeat forgiveness to yourself.

3. What Is the Destiny of Karma?

The link between destiny and karma has already been shown, but you still must see for yourself the patterns of your life. These exercises are designed to help you see the pattern clearly.

Crystal Exercise: Choose three stones from a group of stones and crystals. The first represents the purpose of your karma, the second your hidden feelings about it, the third the training it is giving you. For interpretation, see Table 1.

Visualizing: Imagine the pattern of your life. What structure does it have? How is karma guiding you?

Journal Exercise Write down your karma. What is it teaching you? Try to make sense of the disconnected events of your life. Assuming there is an intelligence guiding your learning process, where does it seem to be going? List the things unhappiness has taught you. List the things happiness has taught you.

Art Exercise: Draw, sculpt, dance, or otherwise express the pattern of your karma.

Game-Playing: Play Smoke with your karma.

Living Well

Fulfilling destiny and discovering karma focus on the individual's uniqueness. But living well is a mission that all of us share. The world and its beauties were not created as a distraction from the spiritual heights. You're supposed to enjoy things, feel emotions, become a whole person. You're supposed to live well; that's what living is for.

What does living well entail? It's easy to give details that fit me but may not fit you; to a certain extent it's a relative concept. It has almost nothing to do with money—except that if you worship money you're likely to miss many of the nonmonetary pleasures you were meant to enjoy. (Why? Because if you worship—or overvalue—money, you'll tend to downplay anything not bought with cash, credit, or traveller's checks. And because the love of money tends toward a kind of paranoia, you'll be so busy wondering if anyone's going to steal your "precious"—see Gollum—that you can't actually enjoy your precious or anything else.)

Living well presupposes a reverential (or at least respectful) attitude toward the world and all created things. If you feel that way, you'll try to understand ecology and live in harmony with the Earth, instead of in warfare with it. You'll be thankful for the riches of the world, from soft cotton woven into patterns to clean water dancing in a waterfall, from sunsets and moonrises to the lightning leaping from cloud to cloud.

Living well can perhaps be understood best by looking at it on different levels. On the physical level, it entails a warm awareness and appreciation of the world, of the goodness of ordinary life, which can be achieved by acknowledging death.

If you were told you had six months to live, you would almost certainly change your life. You would do what you've put off doing; you would change your priorities; you would live with a holy intensity. Rain and sunlight, love and music would take on new and deeper meaning to you; money would probably mean less to you. You would eat plain bread with joy, sensing in every bite the death and resurrection of the grain, the tender sprouts thrusting through the earth, the still hot days of harvest, the baker's floury hands and the long slow rising of the yeast. Your newfound sense of process and purpose would teach you to rejoice and be glad in the bread, and your rejoicing would nourish you. And—since you'd be paying much more attention to what you're eating—you'd probably stop eating tasteless, processed white bread and build yourself up with something closer to Earth and to human hands and skills. You would live well.

The reason our lives are wasted (therefore dull) is that we

forget both that we must die and that we are immortal. Your actions matter: you have all eternity to enjoy—or suffer—the consequences of choices you make today. Your actions matter: you have only the present moment in which to choose, enjoy, act, forgive, because the only certain thing in life is that it will end.

"You cannot kill time without murdering eternity," said Thoreau. Killing time implies boredom and wastefulness—not living well.

Urgency, freshness, and passion are the way we are supposed to live. Your choices of work, your relationships with other people, your willingness to learn and grow and change and forgive, your attitude toward the created Universe and toward the Creator—all are transformed by the realization that what you do matters, every second matters. Are you, now, living with the intensity compelled by our few short years? Andrew Marvell (in "To His Coy Mistress") said it best:

> But at my back I always hear
> Time's winged chariot hurrying near...
> Let us roll all our strength and all
> Our sweetness up into one ball
> And tear our pleasures with rough strife
> Thorough the iron gates of life.

That is living well: with intensity, passion, joy.

On the psychological level, living well means becoming a whole person; doing whatever is necessary to heal yourself and your relationships with other people. All too often, we accept a diminished life, a life devoid of strong emotions. Because we fear pain, we guard ourselves—and thus lock out joy. Enjoyment seems to play a large part in this discussion, but enjoyment isn't the only factor in living well. Willingness to feel the full range of emotions is. True life—lived to its core—

will include a lot of pain, anger, sadness, grief, restlessness, uncertainty, and a host of other forbidden emotions. What do you do with them?

You feel them and you go on. If you repress them, they'll demand expression in another way; emotions are like that. You cannot wall them off without doing yourself damage. If you deny them, after a while you'll stop feeling them; but they'll hide in the psychological level, almost inaccessible, and haunt you in nightmares, in body-image problems, in unexplained depressions, in sick relationships. One way or another, those unacceptable feelings will push for expression. It's far better to feel them, know them, find the source, and go on.

Becoming a whole person also helps heal your relationships with other people. When you are whole, you do not exploit or oppress or abuse others, because you see them as humans. When you're not fully human, no one else is, either. You begin to love your neighbor as yourself; because you can love yourself you can love your neighbor.

And this takes us at last into the most important issue. What is living well on a spiritual level? It is loving God and your neighbor. This is the law and prophets; these essentials lie at the core of all great religions.

The techniques, exercises, and ideas given here are designed to help you know yourself. Knowing the glories and intricacies of the human soul is one way to begin to perceive the Creator, Who has left fingerprints on everything created. But go on from there. The subtlety and majesty and playfulness and goodness of God can be known only through a personal relationship. God rewards the questing spirit, who seeks the Creator, who longs for Jesus, who desires the Inner Light of the Holy Ghost. Without the holy love of God, no life is well lived.

Except the Lord build the house, they labor in vain that build it; except the Lord keep the city, the watchman waketh but in vain. It is vain for you to rise up early, to sit up late, to eat the bread of sorrows, for so he giveth his beloved sheep. (Psalms 127: 1-3)

Notes

1. I should enter a caveat here: I am by no means convinced of the truth of reincarnation. There is evidence for and against it. I do, however, believe in an afterlife, and that our actions and beliefs on Earth determine the nature of that afterlife. Most of all, I believe that you need a relationship with God—an ongoing, breathing, loving, honest dialogue. There are many ways to open yourself to God: ritual and spontaneous prayer, meditation, reading spiritual works, living well, manual labor, and a thousand other ways. Ideally, every moment, act, and thought should be part of that mystical closeness. This kind of personal relation presupposes a personal God, not mere cosmic forces; the deity of Jesus, Who died and was resurrected for our sins; and the constant and loving presence of the Holy Spirit— sometimes called the Inner Light—Who continually tries to draw us closer to God. This is what I believe and what my work is premised upon.
2. The image of layers of plastic is based on Ian McHarg's work, which is used to discover the best sites for new construction. A full—and fascinating—explanation is given in John McPhee's *Coming into the Country* (New York: Farrar, Straus, and Giroux, 1980), "What They Were Hunting For."
3. For some of the history of mazes and some of the designs embedded in them, see the article on mazes in the December 1987 *Smithsonian*.
4. Kelynda, *The Crystal Tree* (West Chester, PA: Whitford Press, 1987).

5. Smoke is a parlor game, but I first heard of it through the writings of the late John Gardner, who used it as a creative-writing exercise. See John Gardner, *On Becoming a Novelist* (New York: Harper & Row, 1983), pp. 32-33. The book was published posthumously; in September 1982 Gardner died on a steep, curving road—the road I grew up on—in Susquehanna County, Pennsylvania, and was buried on the day he was to have been married. He was 49, a great writer whose best work was ahead of him. *Carpediem.*

6. Kelynda, *The Crystal Tree,* pp. 23-28.

7. Ursula K. LeGuin, "The Child and the Shadow," in *The Language of the Night,* ed. Susan Wood (New York: Perigee, 1979). p. 64. I wish I could have quoted the entire essay; it's a clear, thoughtful exploration of the role the Shadow plays in our lives. For a less direct and analytical look at the Shadow, see some of LeGuin's stories, notably "Darkness Box," reprinted in *The Wind's Twelve Quarters* (New York: Harper and Row, 1975). Many of her novels and stories deal with the quest, the labyrinth, the Shadow, the role and meaning of art and music, and the idea of living well. All are worth reading and rereading.

8. All my case histories are based on experiences of my clients, but names and other identifying details have been changed to protect my clients' privacy.

9. Stephen Arroyo, *Astrology, Karma and Transformation* (Davis, CA: CRCS, 1975), p. 6.

10. *The Larousse Encyclopedia of Mythology* (New York: Hamlyn, 1959), p. 326.

11. John 9. The whole chapter is devoted to this remarkable healing and the reactions of those who would not believe it.

Further Reading

These sources are useful for discovering more about yourself and about the spiritual life.

Bolles, Richard Nelson. *What Color Is Your Parachute?* Berkeley: Ten Speed Press, 1987. A marvelous series of exercises designed to help you find out what you want to do.

Faith and Practice. Philadelphia: Philadelphia Yearly Meeting, 1979. The use of queries—questions to ask yourself—is an old Quaker custom. Includes a list of queries that you may find helpful, as well as some meditations and readings.

Fields, Rick, et al. *Chop Wood, Carry Water.* Los Angeles: Jeremy P. Tarcher, 1984. A guide to all aspects of spiritual fulfillment.

Gawain, Shakti. *Creative Visualization.* New York: Bantam, 1982. A brief but essential guide to the techniques and uses of visualizing.

Goldsmith, Joel S. *The Contemplative Life.* Secaucus, NJ: Citadel Press, 1963. An extraordinary and lyrical handbook on meditation and living in the Spirit.

Greene, James, and David Lewis. *Know Your Own Mind.* New York: Rawsom Associates, 1983. A series of tests to determine your skills in different areas.

Lewis, C.S. *Surprised by Joy.* New York: Harcourt, Brace, Jovanovich, 1955. Lewis's autobiography is an excellent introduction to his thought. (If you prefer, you can read the Chronicles of Narnia—all seven volumes—and come to his work that way). Read Lewis for his sense of the holiness and sweetness of ordinary life, the glorious order and pattern of the Universe. He's occasionally sexist, but with so many other spiritual treasures in his work, that can be forgiven. Once you've read this book, go on and read all his others.

Phillips, Dorothy Berkley; Elizabeth Boyden Howes; and Lucille M. Nixon. *The Choice Is Always Ours*. Wheaton, IL: Re-Quest Books, 1982. A series of brief readings in finding the Path. It brings together quotations from many and varied sources, some of them now difficult to find (the original version was published in 1948).

Progoff, Ira. *At a Journal Workshop*. New York: Dialogue House Library, 1975. The Intensive Journal (TM) technique for self-discovery. Progoff also gives workshops using this book as his basic text.

Rainer, Tristine. *The New Diary*. Los Angeles: Jeremy P. Tarcher, 1978. More on journal writing, less intense and more open than Progoff. Both books are very useful.

The Way of a Pilgrim and *The Pilgrim Continues His Way*. Trans. by R.M. French. New York: Seabury Press, 1968. An anonymous classic—originally written in Russian—of the spiritual life.

2 Forgive Yourself

by Edward Sparks

The purpose of this chapter is to transfer the ownership of specific information and concepts from me to you, the reader, and to give you an opportunity to take total responsibility for your life. My goal is to help you become aware of your own inner power and learn to use the power of your higher inner mind to create a new level of self awareness and physical health never before reached, so that you can have a full personal experience of oneness with the God power in your Universe, fully realizing your own magnificence.

The techniques I offer here include creative visualization, affirmation and body cleansing. We will deal with the power of thought and the power of the spoken word, using the energy of the Universe to recreate a lifestyle committed and dedicated to a higher self image, greater self-confidence, improved communication skills, heightened creativity, a prosperity consciousness and an overall increase in personality dynamics. Through the use of these new-found skills you can create a new life now and set up the foundation for rewarding lives in the future.

Forgiveness is the Master Key
Guilt is the Lock

What do you need to do to be able to set up a rewarding future life? How can you prepare for your next life/lives? Obviously, the first step is to take care of this life. Let us start with the two major doors, guilt and karma.

Definition: GUILT (Webster's Dictionary): The fact of having committed a breach of conduct. A feeling of remorse.

Definition: KARMA (Webster's Dictionary): The force generated by a person's actions to perpetuate transmigration and in its ethical consequences to determine his destiny in his next existence.

Translation: GUILT (Edward): Being to blame, being at fault. Not being responsible, not coming from cause.

Translation: KARMA (Edward): A self-imposed condition of having been bad—therefore creating self-imposed punishment over one and/or more lifetimes. A self-imposed condition of having been good, therefore creating self-imposed rewards over one and/or more lifetimes.

We have accumulated a lot of karma and guilt throughout the many lives that we have experienced on the long road of time. Somewhere, somehow we also must have released much karma and guilt. Otherwise, we would be overwhelmed with the effect of pain and suffering. How do we release this garbage we imposed upon ourselves?

The most common is to amass good karma, by performing good works, by developing such virtues as patience and compassion, or by persisting in pursuing worthy goals despite all obstacles. To a degree, good karma can counterbalance bad karma, although the issue is too complex to go into much detail here. However, it is my experience that the deepest source of "bad karma" lies not in the actual "evil deeds," but in the guilt that inevitably follows. The key to the future—the time between what you call now and the rest of your present life—is *forgiveness.*

All great Masters teach that you are the master of your destiny, and the events of your life and/or lives are directly related to the choices and decisions you have made consciously and/or subconsciously, recently or in the distant past. These decisions entail judgments that you are or have been "good" or "bad," based mostly on social and religious conditioning and your environment. If your judgment is that you have been bad, chances are you will manifest guilt and choose a karmic path of pain, unworthiness, self-destruction and being the Victim (everybody hates me so I am going to eat worms!). Your path to a rewarding future is in serious doubt. On the other hand, if you accept this pain and suffering as payback for your past "sins"and declare the debt paid in full, then you may indeed be clearing the way for an unobstructed future. The question is: How much pain must I endure to clean up my bad karma?

Throughout the many regressions and research projects in which I have participated, I have seen a disturbing pattern unfold: we humans tend to punish ourselves at an 8 to 1 ratio, 8 punishing lives for one bad life. This hardly seems just; even the Bible only decrees "an eye for an eye and a tooth for a tooth." So why do our lives seem to express "eight teeth for a tooth?" The answer appears to be that we are assuming much more guilt than our so-called "sins" warrant—and the tendency to reward ourselves for good karma is much less than one would consciously believe.

The bottom line is to *Forgive Yourself NOW.*

This is more difficult than it sounds. The statement, "forgive yourself" is oversimplified. Let us consider what kind of effort this process will take.

Guilt manifests in the human physical body. (Where do you think diseases come from?) Take a close look at your body and your self worth. Look around you. How do you feel about your life—parents, present relationships, childhood, work, your overall well-being?

When you accept the concept taught by the great Masters that you are the Master of your own destiny and you create and manifest your own reality, you will realize that you have and have always had the god-given right and power to forgive yourself. It sounds so simple, yet look around you. Close your eyes and feel the hate you have within you. In your mind you can say "I forgive" and you think that you do—however, the proof is in the result. Look and feel your body. Has it transformed into a picture of perfect health?

Hate, anger and guilt can be hidden deep within, and only when the body is in a *pure state* and in perfect working order will you know that you have rid yourself of hate, anger and guilt. *Your body is the window and door to your soul—and God-self.* Think about this. Your body—and the resulting conditions—that exist now in your life are directly related to your own true self-image and your ability to allow the world around you to exist *just as it is* and to accept the people in your personal reality *just as they are.* Remember, you create your own reality and your own outer world. Therefore, the Universe exists just as it is because you have created it so. Do you like the picture? Would you like to see it change? Would you like to create it another way? Okay, here it comes: The first step is to accept yourself and the world around you just as it is *right now.* Only then can you choose to make changes in it. You must accept the here and now before you can move *forward without karma.*

Forgiving yourself totally is a lot like losing weight. How many diets have you been on? How many times have you said, "I've got to do something about my health—I need to exercise, change my eating habits, treat myself better? What have you actually done toward improving your health?

In my twenty-five years of doing research, seeking the path, asking questions, working with clients, I have found that:

The purer the physical body, the cleaner your karma.

The purer the physical body, the closer your mind/body/soul is to the God Source.

The purer the physical body, the more effect the creating being has upon the Universe as a whole.

The purer the physical body, the more *obvious your ability to forgive yourself.*

The purer the physical body, the easier it is for you to give total and unconditional love to all humankind.

Cleansing Process

1. Totally forgive yourself.
2. Totally release yourself from all guilt.
3. Totally forgive everyone for everything.
4. Hold no grudges.
5. Blame no one for anything.
6. Accept total responsibility.
7. Totally believe in yourself.
8. Accept and be willing to use the God-given power as your own.
9. Accept your own magnificent being as part of God. In other words, give total love with no restrictions.

The Human Body

Science agrees, and experiments have shown, that the body biochemically has the ability to repair itself totally. It can rejuvenate and recreate itself. Therefore, in theory, your body is literally capable of immortality. Thus it logically follows that if your body can be properly cared for, receiving full nutritional value of the foods that it is biochemically designed to process, and all of your glands and organs are able to operate at their full capacity, the only way you could possibly die would be by an accident—and I don't believe there are any, do you? The big question is: Why *don't* we live that long? The answer is simple: We have forgotten how. The only reason we die is that we *think* we are supposed to die and therefore we choose to do so.

The human body is the most perfect machine in the known Universe. The wonders of the human eye, ear and brain are unsurpassed by any known living or non-living thing. But in recent centuries humanity itself has been poisoning these perfect machines. We have been doing this through:

Guilt—not forgiving ourself and/or others;

Stress—work, relationships, peer pressure, parent pressure, lifestyle;

Anger—not allowing the world around us to be as it is;

Eating the wrong sort of foods, foods that our bodies were clearly not designed to process;

Withholding communications—not expressing anger, hate, love.

We read in the Bible about people who lived to be nine hundred years old and more. Some theorists maintain that this is due to confusion between the calendars kept in ancient times and the calendars used now, but I believe that people actually did live that long. Again, according to the Bible, it was only after the Great Flood (known among metaphysicians as the sinking of Atlantis), when vegetation on the Earth was at a minimum and human beings were forced to eat meat or starve, that the lifespan of *homo sapiens* was shortened greatly. (Methuselah lived 965 years while Noah only lived 120.) We then began to die at the commonly accepted limit of "three score and ten."

As the Aquarian Age comes upon us, the minds, bodies and souls of human beings everywhere cry out to transform, to merge as a single unit and form a dwelling place of health and enlightenment. With the uniting of the trinity of the cleansed mind-body-soul, a physical body can be produced that is virtually indestructible and fulfills the concept of total self forgiveness. The cleansing of mind, body and soul creates the condition whereby the individual entity called a human being will become a vessel wherein the Power of God, that which is called BEING, can comfortably reside. The individual then will have the opportunity to accept the responsibility of the return to the Christ Light and a total experience of the God-Self, the Divine "I AM." As we approach the onset of the Aquarian Age, which is the Age of Individuality and the mastery of Total Self and unity with the Universe, the merging of the mind power that dwells on and within the Earth becomes more apparent. As our minds become more and more aware of the infinite nature of their ability, it becomes more and more obvious that we are in control and have total choice in our lives. Therefore, the choice becomes ours whether we should continue to live for an indefinite number of centuries or to leave the planet— not through death, but through a process called "discarnation," meaning that the physical body simply disappears, its atoms becoming scattered among the cosmos, to be reassembled again in other forms. This is the choice that all of us will have when we have reached the level of perfection which we all have the power to achieve.

In perfect working order, the body has the capacity to live beyond eight hundred years. A known scientific fact is that the soft tissues in the body are replaced every seven months, and the hard-celled tissues, as in bone, are replaced every seven years. Cells that do not replace themselves cause a well-known process called aging. When the cells regularly and completely replace themselves, you do not age. Imagine what you could accomplish in eight hundred years! Think of what your CDs would be worth! Imagine the knowledge that you could assimilate with this much time to study, experiment, create careers, travel, love, nurture, give and receive.

Diseases are the result of a damaged ecological cellular environment. Stress is a major disruption to the ecology of the cellular environment, and a harbinger of disease, aging and premature death. The negative chemical environment created by stress causes an actual DNA memory loss. Therefore, cells that would normally recreate themselves perfectly are unable to do so. Nor can they protect themselves from toxins, bacteria and viruses that are ingested into an improperly kept body.

DNA is a scientific term used to describe the substance containing the memories in the chromosomes of all living cells, enabling those cells to reproduce themselves, either to maintain an existing body and/or to create a new one. It is much like a very special computer program designed to keep the body performing at maximum capacity, and unless it is interfered with it will do so. It is my belief that aberrations (weakening) in DNA memory are the source of much of what medical science refers to as disease. If the DNA contained within each cell is perfect, as it was created and as it should be, the body will continue to reproduce itself and maintain perfect health. However, if outside forces such as genetic weakness, air pollution, poor diet or stress put strain on the DNA, the memory contained within it will eventually be lost—hence disease, aging and premature death.

Scientific experiments with rats have shown that almost any type of irritation to living tissue will cause deterioration, stress and an inability of the tissue to recreate itself. In some cases, it actually sets up a condition of runaway cellular reproduction and destruction of healthy living cells. Some people call this cancer.

To say a person has cancer means that cell production in the body has gone out of control and the body cannot fight the unnecessary cell growth. Eventually, the "bad cells" crowd out the "good cells."

The colon is particularly vulnerable to cancer because modern humans have changed the purpose of the body part we call the large intestine and/or colon. The true purpose of the colon is to absorb the nutrition-giving chemicals and enzymes that remain after digestion and then to extract what's left of them from the body. For most modern people, the colon has become the garbage dump of the digestive system, where undigested fermenting and putrefying animal flesh remains for days. Instead of absorbing nutrition, the colon absorbs toxins and poisons—and assists in the karmic work of manifesting pain and suffering.

Another way this imbalance can manifest in the body is Auto-Immune Deficiency Syndrome, or AIDS. Simply stated, AIDS may be defined as the immune system's inability to protect itself and recreate fresh, vital new cells. AIDS has no origin in nature; it is due to the accelerated deteriorating condition of our Earth and the human race as a whole. Though AIDS is blamed on a virus, it appears to be the result of a physiological weakness. Let me attempt to give a common-sense explanation of how AIDS is transmitted and what it is.

Modern society's tendency to live "life in the fastlane" has weakened the human constitution considerably and, consequently, the human race is on the list of endangered species. Let me illustrate. There is a process that occurs in your brain that has been referred to as the "fight-or-flight" reaction. In the early days of *homo sapiens*, this reaction occurred whenever one of our primitive ancestors was chased by a tiger or faced an enemy. The body's rhythms speeded up and adrenalin raced to all parts of the body, enabling the person to either run away or fight. This did put a strain on the body, but how often was a person chased by a tiger or confronted by an enemy? Not often! Most of our early ancestors' time was spent looking for food, which abounded, or relaxing—and so the speeded-up body rhythms did not put too much strain on them. Modern society and its pressures keep the fight-or-flight reaction *turned on all the time.* AIDS, diabetes, heart diseases, brain stroke, and numerous other debilitating ailments are the result.

Although the medical establishment believes that AIDS is caused by a virus, they cannot actually use their instruments to detect the presence of AIDS or the suspected virus. They can only detect antibodies in the blood that show that the body is fighting the condition. It is my belief that AIDS is not caused by bacteria and/or the infamous virus, but is instead loss of memory in the DNA. With the loss of memory the cell loses its ability to protect and re-create itself, and therefore becomes self-destructive. To transmit this type of condition between bodies requires a source that contains a strong DNA concentration (such as blood and/or semen and vaginal fluid). The body to which the imbalance would be transmitted must also be in a weakened condition, one in which the loss of DNA memory has already begun to occur.

When a human body is in optimal working order it is virtually impossible for any form of destructive DNA memories to overwhelm the residing chromosomes and their health-oriented repairing structural memories. The solution, therefore, is to get the human body into near-perfect working order.

Diseases are a result of a weakened human condition and karmic agreement. A well-fed, well-exercised, near-stressless *forgiving* lifestyle can increase humanity's life span tremendously, limited only by your spiritual awareness, enlightenment, willingness to forgive, and to expand your personal limits beyond your wildest imagination.

The Way It Is

As you increase your knowledge and awareness, you will discover that you cannot have, repeat cannot have, everything that you believe you want, but you can have, repeat absolutely can have (and do have) everything that you *believe* you *deserve*. *(Read this paragraph over a few times.)*

If you want to find out what you believe you *deserve,* look at your life just the way it is! Take a good long look at your life and know that this is what you believe you *deserve* and that you have created it accordingly. Somewhere, sometime, you yourself have made a choice and placed limits and restrictions upon yourself so that you cannot proceed any further than a particular level physically, financially, psychologically and emotionally. Where and when did you make this decision? It could have been made in this life and/or past lives, and at some moment in this life the decision was reinforced. Freudian psychologists would contend that you are operating from decisions made in your childhood—and in many cases they are probably right. The craziest thing about this, however, is that the decision may have come from the mind of a three-year-old and have nothing to do with the incident and/or the truth.

Example: A beautiful three-and-a-half year old child has spent the afternoon making mudpies. She greets her father at the front door. The father has had a bad day at the office. Now the little girl is the apple of the father's eye, but at this particular moment, the last thing he wants is mud on his clean pants. When the child makes contact with her father, he overreacts angrily. The child is devastated by this rejection, and in her young inexperienced thought processes, she makes the decision that her father no longer loves her and that she is unworthy of being loved by a man. This can result in a lifetime of unhappy relationships. Such a decision can have its roots in past incarnations, and be reinforced at the moment of rejection by the father. Ridiculous, isn't it? But it happens *all the time!*

When you seek the source of this life's problems, you should realize that most likely you are operating out of past karma and decisions made in past lives. Let me define karma again. Karma is a decision that you made after a traumatic event (traumatic event being of your own personal choice) of some sort that has placed limitations upon your level of accomplishment in some way. It is a judgment that you have done something bad or wrong, thus making you believe that you deserve punishment of some sort. On the other hand, if you feel that what you have done is correct, appropriate and good, you will reward yourself. The way to break the pattern is simply to understand that you are in a position of choice at all times, and to fully believe that "I deserve a complete, loving, nurturing, rewarding relationship, and I forgive myself for all my past indiscretions and bad and evil doings. I accept the responsibility for whatever I did, whenever I did it, and it's over with now. I FORGIVE MYSELF." (This makes a very good mantra and/or affirmation.)

You are constantly, consistently, in agreement with yourself, and at any given moment in time, you have the right and the power to rearrange and renegotiate this agreement with yourself. You don't like the limits and restrictions you have placed upon yourself? Then stop playing the victim (give up eating worms) and take responsibility. Raise your goals. Create new goals and go for it!!! Shoot for the stars! Stop being an I CAN'T person. If you took your portion of the Universe and converted it into a monetary system, you would not be able to spend it all in a hundred lifetimes. This and more is how much you own in the Cosmos. So why are you playing with nickles and dimes? What will it take for you to break away from the self-imposed parameters and self-limiting statements and attitudes that you have been living under as if your life depended on them?

Here are some new attitudes that you might consider adapting into your life as if your life depended on them.

Adjust/Adapt/Improvise

ADJUST: *For things to change you must change.* By changing your attitudes and beliefs, you will enable things around you to change. You must adjust to fit any given circumstance without experiencing a sense of losing something. The adjustment must be a win-win condition. When creating a win-win condition, you also must create a willingness to surrender to that condition without stress. Let Go and Let God.

ADAPT: *For things to get better you must get better.* A willingness to adapt into any circumstance or situation gives you the power of control. By allowing yourself to relinquish the attitude *"I must win at any cost"* you always create a condition of win-win. By allowing others to receive what they want, you get what you want.

IMPROVISE: *For things to move you must move.* The ability to call upon your inner self to provide the tools of creating choice, without producing damage to the environment and/or emotional conditions around you, gives you the secrets to adaptation and adjustment.

Know When to Break and to Make Up Your Own Rules

Among the greatest tools of adjust, adapt and improvise is knowing when to break the rules without causing damage to the environment and/or emotional conditions around you, while still maintaining your integrity. For example, would you break the speed law of 55 miles per hour to save the life of someone you love? If you needed a job and knew that the company you were applying to wanted to hire people younger than yourself, would you lie about your age? The danger here is being reasonable. When you are reasonable you are not always realistic.

To be realistic, and still maintain your integrity, can be very difficult. Remember, you are the guiding force in your life and when you choose to accept the responsibility of virtually anything, then and only then can you renegotiate with your higher self and/or God (your choice) a new agreement that is much more satisfying and nurturing to a lifestyle you *desire* and *definitely deserve*.

Beware of Self-Imposed Parameters and Self-Limiting Statements and Attitudes

"I can't" is arsenic to your life. Accepting the responsibility that throughout your lifetime, consciously and/or subconsciously you have imposed and locked yourself into parameters that keep you from growing and expanding into the person that you are and *deserve* to be. Accept the responsibility that consciously and/or subconsciously, throughout your lifetime you have made specific statements about yourself that limit your growth and expansion. Become aware of words that take away, restrict, limit and kill a part of you, words like *I can't-I'll try-I need-never-hate-impossible-hope* (make your own list and learn it well). By becoming aware of your self-imposed limits on a conscious level, you can set up a countering condition, by releasing your parameters and continuously making positive and nurturing statements to and about yourself. One of the quickest ways to do this is to use subliminal tapes which are designed to reinforce your self-image, self confidence, creativity and personality dynamics. Another very simple technique is to create a simple affirmation, something as simple as "I Can," "I Am OK," "I Love Myself," "I Deserve a Loving and Nurturing Relationship." You can say these rhythmically and repetitively a hundred or more times while driving or walking. When looking into the bathroom mirror, repeat your chosen affirmation,

eyeball to eyeball with your inner "guru." (This has a
particularly powerful effect.)

Become Aware of When You Accept Parameters and Limitations from Others

As you become aware of self-limiting conditions, you also need
to become aware of when you are allowing yourself to accept
any limitations and parameters imposed upon you by others.
Divorce yourself from the idea that standing up for your rights
is disrespectful. When you feel and believe that others are
attempting to limit you through manipulations—*Let 'em help-
you can't do that-you need me-that's impossible*—realize that
you are not doing yourself or them any favors by allowing
them to do so. If you let the activity continue, you are allowing
your friends to build bad karma. Here is a good opportunity to
apply the laws of *adjust/adapt/improvise*.

Become Aware When You Adjust Your Actions to Fit the Beliefs of Others

This is a condition that I consider extremely dangerous and
self-limiting. Any time you enter into a condition to please
someone else that compromises your beliefs and your
integrity, you are invalidating who you are and losing that part
of yourself some call God. *Be Yourself.*

Notice When You Change Your Normal Behavior Patterns for Certain People

Become aware of the difference between respect and blind
worship. Make an agreement with yourself that it is okay for

other people to *disagree* with your belief system and it is okay for you to disagree with their belief systems. This will not damage the emotional environment or infringe on others' beliefs. Be more cautious when someone insists that what you believe in is wrong and what they believe is the *only* truth, the *only* way. You must choose for yourself what is right and wrong. Only you can truly know.

The Importance of Making and Keeping Agreements

When you make agreements, either oral or written, with yourself or with others and particularly in the great Cosmos, you are creating a very special energy. Accept the concept that an agreement is something that you enter into as if your life depended on it. Keeping your agreements is one of the most important things you can do to promote a healthy lifestyle and body. When you *keep* an agreement, you create a win-win condition. When you *break* an agreement without renegotiation, you create a negative energy that must be cleaned up as quickly as possible by renegotiating a win-win condition that both parties accept. Remember that you have the right at any time to renegotiate any agreement. And here is where a universal law applies. The renegotiations must produce a win-win situation just as if the original agreement had been fulfilled. Keep your appointments. Don't be late. Keep your word. Fulfill your promises.

Attitude and Disease

What Do Agreements Have to Do with Diseases?

When an agreement is made and kept, an energy of fulfillment is created and released. When an agreement is broken, a condition of disrupting energy is created (guilt). This disrupting energy can and will cause serious, negative chemical changes within the body and mind which, depending upon the importance of the agreement, can and will cause serious damage now and/or in the future to the individual breaking the agreement. It will also create emotional damage to the environment of the relationship of the parties involved in the agreement. This negative energy will cause cellular disruption, thus allowing a condition in which disease and/or diseases flourish.

Here is the Catch-22 of agreements. No matter what you do, where you go, who you do it to, who does it to you, you cannot and never can *not be* in The Agreement. Only you can create the energy of a broken agreement. You create for yourself by choosing positive or negative conditions. Being right or wrong is *your* choice and it's a choice of life or *death*.

What Does Anger Have to Do with Diseases?

When you are angry, the adrenal gland secretes adrenaline, which creates an abundance of physical energy and extreme nervousness. When you experience anger and fear and do not release the anger in a *positive* manner and/or hold the anger inside, a *negative* energy many times more powerful than the negative energy created by breaking an agreement is produced. Breaking an agreement can produce anger. In extreme cases, unreleased anger will create some form of disease: cancer, heart condition, stroke, etc.

Learning to express your anger without creating damage to others, the environment or the emotional conditions surrounding you is vital to your health and life. Once again, here is an opportunity to apply the laws of adjust/adapt/improvise.

Let us look at some ways to release your anger without doing any damage or disruption to others. If you are healthy enough, running and expressing yourself verbally while you're running is effective. I also recommend punching a punching bag, swimming (I've been known to shout at the ocean!) or engaging in some other physical activity in order to burn off the adrenaline and relieve the tension and stress. It is not necessary to express the anger you feel in the direction of the person you think gave you the opportunity to be angry. If you use finesse, you can verbalize that you are angry and thank that person for the opportunity to handle it. Doesn't this sound like fun?

How Do Relationships Affect Diseases?

Relationships engage our emotions and our emotions constantly change the chemistry of our bodies. These chemical changes can be either positive or negative, thus creating a condition of healing or cellular disruption (which promotes the possibility of disease). In any relationship between two human beings, communication and the form that it takes, verbal and/or non-verbal, can result in a positive or negative chemical reaction.

In the Aquarian Age, telling the truth is one important factor in a relationship. However, bear in mind that when you tell the blatant, unvarnished truth regardless of the results, you can produce a condition that is not fulfilling and/or nurturing to the individual you are communicating to, or to yourself. With a little bit of forethought, you can always tell the truth in such a manner that it creates a win-win situation and sets up a positive chemical reaction that promotes healing and bonding in the relationship.

At times, I have been known to tell the unvarnished, blatant truth without regard for the other person's environment. To my dismay, I realized too late that I created a damaging situation. Now when I become aware that I have done this, I immediately seek an opportunity to repair and re-create my truths in a more positive and nurturing manner. When I do this, I experience an incredible feeling of success and accomplishment. Take a look at your relationships, particularly your recent ones. Most likely there are great opportunities for you to re-create the communications and enjoy feelings of accomplishments and success, too. This definitely is having fun with life!

The Importance of Attitude and Diseases

Attitudes and physiology cause chemical changes within the human body. These chemical changes can be either positive or negative, and thus create either a condition of healing or of cellular disruption and disease.

Physiology is the position and attitude of your body. Its condition and expression, your movements, the way you stand, the way you hold your arms, how you place your weight over your feet all affect the chemistry of your body. This is also a form of non-verbal communication. Example: Crossing your arms when talking to someone. Your crossed arms represent your resistance to communication. By simply *uncrossing* your arms and/or legs you change the chemistry in your body so that it becomes more positive and nurturing. Be aware of yourself, and your body positions and language. You can control your entire life and health just by becoming aware of your physical attitude and physiology. *Open Your Body.*

Look at your body. Are you skinny, average, overweight, or just plain fat? Let's consider obesity for a moment. Why do some people who eat a lot get fat? Some people who eat a lot never gain an ounce! You are not only what you eat, but also your image of yourself. Your mental picture of yourself determines how your body will hold and store food. Obese people manifest their poor self-images by creating that wall of fat between society and themselves. The other extreme, the anorexic, believes "I am not worthy to take up space and am attempting to disappear."

Fear and guilt are usually the motivating factors behind overeating. These emotions can lead you to attempt to build a shield or fence around you to protect yourself, either to keep people out or to make a place for you to hide.

I used to be overweight (I weighed 225 pounds). I had created the barrier of my abdomen, which my friends affectionately (and sometimes not so affectionately) called my Buddha belly. It was not easy for me, an ex-Marine whose childhood ambition was to be a big, tough soldier, to admit that I had placed that Buddha belly there because I was afraid of the people around me! But it was true. I now understand that the little round pouch was only a false shield; it never really gave me any security. Once I accepted this, I began to handle my weight (at this writing I am 180 pounds and falling). I constantly remind myself that in the words of John F. Kennedy, the only thing I have to fear is fear itself.

Now whenever I stand in front of an audience, I can accept that a part of me will always be afraid, afraid that I will not be able to speak, or that I will not be accepted by you, or even that you will laugh at the things which I so fervently believe. Somebody might ask me a question that I will not be able to answer. However, this fear goes away the moment that I realize that it does not matter, so long as I come from believing in what I do and say. I also like to tell my audiences that it is okay for them either to agree or disagree with me. If what I say works for your mind, welcome to the club. I give it to you freely and totally with complete love and no restrictions or limitations. Hence, I no longer need the barrier of my Buddha belly.

Words and the Energies They Create

In the beginning was the Word, and the Word was with God, and the Word was God. (John 1:1) This quote has an absolute bearing on your personal health. The words that we use in our daily communications have an effect upon our body chemistry. Unfortunately, we humans are *not* trained by our present society to promote ourselves as positive, nurturing, successful and prosperous beings. Examples: When someone gives you a compliment, do you sheepishly smile and say, "Oh. Thank you," while somewhere inside your head a little voice says, "It's not true"? Yet somewhere else a little voice says, "I wish it were true."

As you can see, this definitely does not promote self-confidence, a positive self-image, and a winning attitude. Please tell me where it is written that you are not a good person? The Bible says that the Meek shall inherit the Earth. What is the definition of the word Meek? It does not mean a low self-confidence, a negative self-image. The word in the Greek Bible which the King James Version's translators interpreted as "meek" literally means, "those who surrender." In other words, those who let go and let God. My personal interpretation of the term "meek" is not damaging, causing grief or creating any negative conditions to myself and/or other human beings. When I live by this philosophy I have the right to do virtually anything in the Universe that I so choose and to have virtually anything that I believe I can have.

Words that kill: I can't—I'll try—I need—never—hate—impossible—hope—practical—almost—bad-wrong—if—don't know—I need to know—should have—shouldn't have. (I can't overstate the importance of making a list to assist yourself in becoming aware of these killing words and how and when you use them.)

Words of health and power: I love—I forgive—I can—I will—I give.

The Importance of Childhood Decisions

Scientists cannot agree when the process called thought begins within the human fetus. My personal belief and observation is that thinking begins when the thing called soul/self enters the growing and developing fetus. I believe the age that this occurs depends upon the agreement between mother and child, and not until this moment of entry does the fetus become a true being. Notice I say that the moment at which the human fetus becomes a thinking, sentient being depends upon the agreement between mother and child. And this varies tremendously from agreement to agreement. With one mother-child pair, this process could begin with conception. With another, it might not begin until the actual moment prior to birth.

There are no rules—only agreements. So begins the decision-making process. This process is an incredible source of energy. As with all energies, these particular ones can be positive and/or negative. As outlined in previous paragraphs, energies created by the mind have a direct effect on human chemistry and thus on the physical body.

More About Agreements

Life is not unlike a play in which you are the writer, the producer, director, and leading character. In this play, you can ad lib or change the entire script, change the scenery and rearrange the agreement at any given moment. How? It's simple. All it takes is the realization that you have choice in your life and are willing to be totally responsible for creating yourself and your life as it is, that you are willing to believe you have the power given by God to move onward and upward to whatever place in the Universe you wish to be. Part of your intellect, or Higher Self, never forgets, and is as old as Time itself.

As we move forward in life, we watch ourselves hit the wall of limitation and we think we have failed. What I am about to tell you is no secret, yet at the same time it is probably the best-kept secret you will ever hear and/or read. I almost feel that I should write this in a whisper. There is no failure. There is only complete and total success at the level that you have agreed to in the overall Agreement. You can never fail and you can never break the Agreement. On second thought, it should be shouted! There is no failure. There is only complete and total success at the level that you have agreed to in the overall Agreement. You can never fail and you can never break the Agreement.

You can only keep your agreements and do what you do when you do it. Anything else is judgment, evaluation, restriction and limitation. These are all made up and are only real when you *believe* that they are real. *Guilt* is a made-up emotion which gets in the way of understanding the Agreement that you can never be right or wrong, you can only keep the Agreement.

Example: Once upon a time there was a man by the name of Adolph Hitler. This man entered into an agreement with a very large portion of the population of the Jewish world. He created for them a space in time and the physical world where they could participate in their karma at a level of suffering. Thus the concentration camps of Nazi Germany were born. If you think about it, one of the most amazing things about the concentration camps is that some of the Jews totally accepted their fate and went to their suffering and deaths in the gas chambers like lambs to the slaughter. Some of them were not in the agreement and never experienced the concentration camps. Others were partially involved in the agreement and escaped death but not some of the suffering of the concentration camps. Now this pain and death *created an energy,* and because all these people were willing to accept the karma, the energy of payment deserved a reward. Thus was born the State of Israel.

Was Hitler right or wrong, good or bad? Or did he merely keep his Agreement and all the people who participated with him keep their agreements and play the game appropriately? They chose to be who they were, where they were, and to do what they did; they had passed a judgment evaluation upon themselves that this is what they deserved.

This is not to be interpreted as a license to kill or harm others. Even though Hitler was in agreement with the Jewish people he is still bound by the laws of cause and effect, and most metaphysicians believe that he will have to pay off karma for every one of the six million lives that he was responsible for taking. *Unless he can accept total forgiveness for himself.*

Another example is Charles Manson. When interviewed by her lawyer, Manson devotee Susan Atkins said that she and the others killed Sharon Tate, Jay Sebring and their friends "because it was their karma to be murdered." They were right. However, Manson and his followers were not completely free to murder whomever they wished simply because they assumed it was the victim's karma and destiny. At any time, they could have chosen not to participate in this manner and found a way instead to create good karma.

The point is to bring it home to you that you have chosen to be where you are right now. I believe that my job in life is to inform you that your Messiahs are dead, that Santa Claus is a myth, and the Easter Bunny was eaten for dinner (by a carnivore, of course). If you want to meet your Saviour, try looking in the bathroom mirror. This is always my favorite part. I, and any other teacher or guru, am only an *instrument* in your life, a key to your memory, the slayer of your Santa Clauses. When you begin to understand that no Messiah, no Santa Claus, no Ascended Master, no UFO is going to come down out of the sky and solve all the world's problems, you take responsibility and learn to rely only on yourself. "Let there be peace on Earth, and let it begin with—*guess who?*" If some of you still wish to keep thinking that there are outside deities, and other gods to worship, then we are also in agreement that you get to believe anything you wish. At this time, however, I would like to introduce you to your true Master Guru. Since the story has it that this Superguru's light is blinding, please close your eyes. (Read this first! Better yet, have someone else read it to you.) Hold out your hands in front of you, elbows bent. Placing your hands together, move them up and down. You are now shaking the hand of your Master Guru. Say hello!

You are the creator, you are the power.

Accidents

Let's talk about *accidents*. If there is only the Agreement, then it stands to reason that there are no accidents. Let's say you are driving down the street, and someone runs a red light and smashes into your car, breaking your back and paralyzing you from the hips down. Suppose his windshield shatters and glass flies into his eyes, blinding him. How did this come to be?

Let's go back in time to that moment before you were born and you were writing the script for your life. Here among millions of minds in the vast cosmic Universe, you made the decision that in your up and coming life, you deserved to be paralyzed from the hips down for the last thirty-five years of your life, and you put this information out into the great cosmic mind, and someone else said, "I'm going to be in that area about that time. I am going to take my sight away from me when I am sixteen years old, so I will meet you at the corner of Main and Broadway and I will run the red light, crashing into your car, breaking your back, shattering my windshield and destroying my eyes." *The Agreement has been cast.* Now do you have to keep this Agreement? *Absolutely! Unless* it is renegotiated. Let me say again that the moment you realize that the Agreement of life is totally a choice, you become completely in control of your life and your destiny. You simply will drive a little slower at the "appointed" time for some unknown reason and the other car will either miss you completely or not hit you in such a way that you are injured. Thus you agree to assist him in his karma, but you have changed yours. You may even choose to be missed completely by him and, if he still wishes, he will find another way to destroy his eyes.

In the moment called *NOW,* and what you do with it, lies the Agreement. We all do this. Sometimes it is very difficult to separate a longtime agreement with an instant choice Agreement. *You cannot lie, cheat, steal, kill or be killed, be lied to, cheated or stolen from unless the Agreement is there.* You are the Master of your destiny. You create your own reality. You create the Universe around you and the Agreement is that we create together, producing each other and the world we live in. Your power is unlimited. It may appear that I have just given you a license to steal; the question is, can you do it without *guilt?*

For quite some time, I have openly and consciously been in an Agreement with the Universe that I would not participate in the taking of a human life. So far, the Agreement has been kept. Example: While driving down a street in El Paso, Texas, either from the corner from my eye or from precognitive awareness (seeing into the future) I saw a small blond girl dash out of the front door of her house, down the sidewalk and into the street between two parked cars. Before she cleared the cars I had locked all four wheels and skidded to a halt with her hands touching my right headlight and fear blazing in her eyes. My heart in my throat, my hand shaking, I rolled down the window and, in a voice mixing anger with relief, I said, "I am sorry, little girl; I refuse to participate in your karma. If you still choose to kill yourself, choose someone else; I am not available." An incredible thing happened. Upon the face of this child was the expression of a full-knowing-exactly-what-I-am-doing person, who understood that I had just instantly renegotiated an agreement!

When I wrote the play and made the agreement is not important. The important thing is that I believe that I have written my life's drama (and I do so love my drama), in which I participate with all of you from my personal perspective of author, playwright, producer and director. The neatest thing of all is that I can at any moment renegotiate and rewrite the script. *I am very clear that I can at any moment renegotiate and rewrite the script and maintain my integrity.*

In my life, little dramas like this are not uncommon. Nor are they in yours. Why and how do they happen? I believe they happen because I have declared to the power of the Universal Divine Energy that I acknowledge the right to renegotiate any agreement that I choose and to create my life as I so choose. The taking of a human life and/or participating in causing harm to anyone at any time for any cause is not acceptable. This is the basis for my personal *prime directive.*

How Can You Influence Your Future Lives?

Everything you do influences your future lifetimes. The goal is to influence them in a positive, nurturing, life-enhancing, way. And that begins now, with cleaning up your present life, by clearing away blocks in your current life, by choosing to live the life you can have and are entitled to have.

Following are some basic tools you may use to assist yourself on your quest. Some are available in audio cassette or fullpage print out.

One Axiom

When you believe you can, and when you believe you cannot, you are always right.

Two Ways to Get Along with Yourself

1 Be true to yourself and your beliefs
2 Make healthy, positive, life-affirming agreements and keep them

Three Ways to Increase Your Energy (Fatigue Makes Cowards of Us All)

1 Choose to have energy
2 Fake it until you have it
3 Do what needs to be done to get it

Four Rules for Handling Commitments

1 Do what must be done
2 Be willing to pay the price
3 Give it your all
4 Never quit

Five Keys to Personal Achievement

Know what you want the outcome to be, then visualize it and affirm for it clearly. Well-defined outcomes are:

1 Stated in a positive manner
2 Stated in detail
3 Given a time frame
4 Have actions and procedures described in detail
5 Cause no harm in any way to the environment or any living being

Six Steps to Creating Good Rapport

1 Check your physiology (create an open body posture)
2 Check the other person's physiology (look for an open body posture)
3 Be aware of your breathing
4 Pay attention to the other person's breathing
5 Clear your mind of negative thoughts
6 Give others what they want

Seven Things I Know to Be True

1 For *things* to change *you* must change
2 For *things* to get better *you* must get better
3 Physiology is the key and leverage to emotional and chemical changes in the human body
4 Knowledge is the antidote to ignorance and fear
5 Thoughts are energy
6 The spoken word creates energy
7 The written word solidifies energy

Eight Ways to Get What You Want in Life

1 Know what you want
2 Ask for it with clarity
3 Be specific
4 Be committed
5 Be tenacious; never give up
6 Believe you deserve
7 Believe in yourself
8 Give others what they want

Forgiving Agreement

I _____ Do Hereby Choose To Totally And Absolutely Forgive (name person) _____. For Any Transgressions And/Or Negative Experiences That I Personally Feel That S/He Caused. I _____ Totally Accept The Fact That I Create My Own Reality And That As The Master Of My Own Reality I Can Therefore Choose To Have The Results That Will Nurture Me And Be Positive Experiences In My Life. I _____ Can Therefore Allow Myself To Be Totally Forgiven For Any Negative Results And Damage To The Personal Ecology Of Any Individual. I Hereby Accept On This Date Of _____/_____/_____ The Total Responsibility Of The Act Of Complete Forgiveness Of (name person) _____ And Upon Any Reoccurence Of The Memory And/Or Negative Reaction Do Hereby Make It Acceptable And OK To Repeat The Total Forgiveness Of This Individual.

SIGNED _____

DATE _____/_____/_____

Witnessed If You Choose

_____

_____

_____

Formal Agreement To Have A Healthy Body

I _____ Do Solemnly Swear On This Day Of _____/_____/_____ That I _____ Right Now At This Moment At _____. _____ AM—PM Do Hereby

Take Total Responsibility For Having Created My Body As It Is Right Now. I _____ Completely And Absolutely Forgive Myself For Any And All Transgressions Upon My Body Done By Me. As Of This Moment In The Time Called Now, My Body And I Are Complete With Each Other. I _____ Choose To Accept The Responsibility Of The Care, Feeding And Cleaning Of This Body Both Inside And Out.

I _____Will Under No Circumstances Injest And Otherwise Put Into My Body Any And All Food Stuffs That Will Cause Harm And Damage And Or Will Alter My Physical And Mental Health In A Negative Way. In No Way Or Form Will I Ever Put Into My Body Mind-Alernating Drugs, Alcohol, Refined Sugars, Tobacco, Excessive Salt, The Flesh Of Any Dead Animal, Fowl Or Fish, The Body Product Of Any Animal. To Support My Body I Will Become Well Educated In What Is Healing And Healthful For My Body. I _____ Will Exercise And Otherwise Keep My Body Moving Toward A Strong And Healthful Condition.

I _____Will Stretch And Otherwise Keep My Body And Mind Reaching Toward A Strong And Healthful Goal. Having Read And Now Understanding That The Above Is About My Life, I Totally Accept Without Any And All Reservations The Complete Commitment And Responsibility Of The Care And Feeding And The Overall Commitment To My Life's Health. I _____Hereby Make This Formal Commitment And Agreement To Myself And God And Accept The Knowledge That My Life Depends On It.

SIGNED _____

DATE _____/_____/_____

Witnessed If You Choose

_____

_____

Tape record the following processes or have someone read them to you.

Re-Enactment Of Love Process

Take a moment and go within yourself and choose an incident from your past when you felt loved. Close your eyes. Visualize the incident. With your mind's eye create in front of you a large panoramic screen. As you see this screen, bring upon it in living color the incident which you have chosen. Now as the author of your life, producer and director, you can at any moment renegotiate with yourself and the Universe. Therefore, as the incident begins to play upon the screen begin to feel that love growing within you. Now allow that feeling of love to increase, growing stronger and stronger. Continue to feel that love growing within you. Now allow that feeling of love to increase. Bathe yourself in love, feel that love within you, and all around you. Now change the screen and continue to maintain this great feeling of love.

Now choose an incident from your past when you felt no love, when you felt alone, depressed, in pain. You know the one. Just for a brief moment in time allow that bad feeling to be. Just as the bad feeling begins to exist, bathe it in that great feeling of love and experience it desolving, and going away and leaving your life forever. Here is an opportunity to recreate your life and have all win-win situations between you and all participants.

Re-enactment Process

Take a moment and go within yourself and choose an incident from your past that you feel created an upset and/or a confusion that felt negative. Close your eyes and visualize the incident. With your mind's eye create in front of you a large panoramic screen. As you see this screen, bring upon it in living color the incident which you have chosen. Now as the author of your life, producer and director, you can at any moment renegotiate with yourself and the Universe. Therefore, as the incident begins to play upon the screen change the energy into a positive and nurturing experience and have the ending come out happy. Use the forgiveness agreement at any time during the re-enactment of the event. Here is an opportunity to recreate your life and establish win-win situations between you and all participants.

I Am Immortal

I AM IMMORTAL
I was born at the beginning of time; I have lived, loved cried
and died numerous lives;
Kings and Queens have bowed to me;
Beggars and thieves have spat upon me.

I AM IMMORTAL
Of lives and loves have I known and been;
Children of Greatness have I begotten;
Beggars and thieves have I sired;
The color of my skin has been all;
Of the countries I have known, worldwide have they
been.

I AM IMMORTAL
Throughout history have I walked as male and
female; have I gone seeing history, living history and
making history;

I AM HISTORY
To live, to love and to grow,
To be born and to die is my destiny,
For God made.........ME.

3 The Moebius Strip of Time

by Brad Steiger

Can we see into the future? I am convinced that I managed three or four times to catch fleeting glimpses of future events in my life. Interestingly, the snatches of tomorrow I viewed were of minor importance.

In one instance, some years ago, I had a dream in which I was standing in the upstairs of my parents' home. My two sons were with me, and we were, for some reason, standing in the dark. From somewhere in the distance, I could hear my mother's voice shouting: "Geese! Hear the geese. They're flying south for the winter!"

At the time, I pondered the symbolism in such a dream. What could it be telling me about my life, my future, my relationships? Were geese symbolic of the wild spirit struggling to break loose within me and fly into new areas of life?

I did not spend a great deal of energy attempting to discover the secret meaning of the dream. I soon forgot about the flight of the geese and the darkened upstairs of my parents' home, and I went about the business of meeting book deadlines and preparing seminars.

It wasn't until several weeks later that I stood in the upstairs of my parents' home, speaking with my sons, who were at that time about fifteen and thirteen years old. We were standing in my old room, looking through some mementos of my youth, when I noticed that it was getting late. The holiday weekend was coming to a rapid close, and it was time for us to start driving home.

I shut out the light, and we stood for a moment in the darkness. Suddenly we heard a series of unusual sounds, a musical honking.

My mother, who was downstairs, could identify the sounds. "The geese. They're flying south for the winter."

I experienced a bizarre tickling sensation in the pit of my stomach as the precise details of the dream were dislodged from my memory. I had had a dream of the future—but what a peculiar slice of it to dream about!

Though the event may seem trivial, the aspect of the greater reality that it represents is staggering. It demonstrates that we do have the ability to foresee the future, and it shows that such talents are best employed while we are in a heightened state of awareness or in an altered state of consciousness, such as a dream, a vision, a trance, a meditative state, or a hypnotic sleep. Over the course of more than thirty years of research, I have developed numerous techniques that permit anyone to develop the ability to mind-travel to the past or to the future.

Once, live on television, I participated in an experiment during which we sent a subject back to the day of Lincoln's Gettysburg Address. The details the subject brought back confounded a number of Lincoln scholars who were present.

During an intensive period of research from 1966 to 1969, I cooperated in an ongoing program during which we hypnotically regressed dozens of men and women into memory patterns strongly suggestive of past-life experiences. In some instances, we were so successful that we were able to locate birth certificates, death certificates, land grants, deeds, and other official records to substantiate the physical reality of our subjects' prior existences on the Earth plane.

Our research group went on to explore the fascinating question of what happens to the soul between lives, and we began to amass some astounding data in this controversial area.

Early in 1968, one of the historians in our advisory board, a college professor with a number of important published works to his credit, suggested that since we had accomplished a good record of convincing trips to the past, we should now attempt progressions into the future.

To the professor's amazement, our volunteer subjects were remarkably successful at slipping into the future. We began our experiments by hypnotically projecting them two or three days ahead on the time track. This had the advantage of being relatively quick and easy to verify. We were, after all, conducting serious tests and it was necessary to receive meaningful feedback as readily as possible. Future projections to the year 2050, for example, would have been meaningless to our research program, for an accuracy check would lie 80 years in the future.

Those early experiments in future projections were very exciting. We felt as though we were pioneers exploring unknown vistas of the psyche. And as I have already suggested, it was during this intensive period of research that I formulated so many of the techniques, exercises, and creative visualizations that I have now utilized in countless seminars, workshops, and lectures.

As I have often stated in the past-life seminars that I have conducted, "There is only one reason to explore past lives: to gain additional tools of awareness that can make your present life more productive."

The same is true of exploring future lives. In my opinion, the only reason to do so is to bring back ideas, skills, talents, and knowledge from that future life so that you may use them to enrich your present life.

Some Experiments in Mind-Travel

To illustrate, let me share more of my experiments in future-lives projection.

A high school athlete came to me upon the advice of his coach. The athlete—we'll call him Gary—had been ill and became despondent. The reasons behind his depression were unclear, but he was greatly troubled. Though he had been ill for only a few days, when he returned to the track squad, where he was a champion pole vaulter, he could no longer perform anywhere near his former standards. Quite naturally, the coach was also troubled by his star athlete's inability to perform to capacity, for the conference championship was only a few days away.

Gary proved to be an excellent subject for hypnosis, and I soon placed him in a deep altered state of consciousness. I moved him ahead to the day of the conference track meet, and I allowed him to experience that time in the future with all of his senses. Mentally, I placed the pole in his hands and let him feel each of the major muscle groups come into play as he began to race down the track toward the bar. I suggested that he figuratively become an eagle and fly over the bar with the ease of the giant bird. As Gary soared over the bar in future time, he did so with the assurance that he had set a conference record. I instructed him to rise from the sand pit and to lift his arms in recognition of the cheers from the crowd.

Although it may sound like the scenario for a television movie of the week, Gary returned to practice a flying tiger and in a few days set a new conference record for the pole vault. By moving him only a very short way into the future, I was able to bring him back flushed with the full knowledge of the victory that would soon be his.

So you want to argue that what I really did was to instill a new sense of confidence in Gary? I am a pragmatic mystic. You will get no debate from me. The point that I am making is that I used the mechanism of traveling into the future and permitting my subject to bring back an accomplishment that most certainly enriched his life. Would you ask Gary to return his trophy over such a moot point?

When my daughter Kari was running for president of her class, she came to me with a bad case of nervousness. She had to make her campaign speech before her assembled class-mates that next morning, and she had the jitters.

I shared with her a technique that I employ when I am nervous before a crowd or just prior to an important meeting. I visualize myself in the future remembering the speech or the encounter. I see myself in a pleasant and comfortable setting, telling a cirlce of close friends how successful the event was for me and my audience.

In other words, whatever the stressful event may be in the present, some day in the future it will be in the past. And in the sense of the Eternal Now, it has already happened, so why worry?

If you employ such a mental mechanism, then it will not matter if you split your trousers or forget your speech. Even such an unpleasant occurrence will, given the healing balm of time, become a humorous anecdote to share with your friends in the future.

Think of all the horrible experiences in your adolescence, think of all those ghastly encounters over which you loudly declared that you would have preferred death or banishment rather than face. How many of them have you since converted into outrageous tales of slapstick comedy for the amusement of your friends?

When Sarah came to me for a hypnotic session, she requested the exploration of a particular past-life experience. She had seen in her personal visions that she had been a superb artist in that life. Though she was presently earning an adequate living as a commercial artist, she yearned to support herself solely through serious artistic expression. In her own periods of contemplation, she felt that she could recall abilities and skills beyond her present level of accomplishment. She wished to travel into the purple mist of time and locate the past life of artistic expertise.

After I had placed Sarah in a deep altered state, I did what I always do: I asked the Source of All That Is to grant that Sarah be able to see that which she needed to see for her good and for her gaining. When I asked the entranced subject to describe her surroundings, it soon became clear to me that she was envisioning a future time. True, she was once again a painter, but the skills and abilities that she had sensed in her own trips through time and space were the products of soul evolution and were the experiences of a future, rather than a past, life experience.

What Sarah was able to bring back with her was a particular method of blending her oils and acrylics with other elements that I cannot disclose. This technique enables her to manifest a liveliness of color and texture that makes her paintings truly unique.

Benefits of Exploring Future Lives

The awareness of a future life has permitted many troubled men and women to free themselves of the anguish and anxiety of their present lives and to progress into the productive and positive aspects of their future lives without undergoing the transition of physical death.

There really is no need for anyone to continue to languish in a lifetime of negative programming. It is possible to begin to structure your future self today.

In 1972, I met Patricia-Rochelle and Jon-Terrance Diegel, an attractive husband-and-wife team who were hosting what they termed "Cosmic Mandate" conferences throughout the United States. Jon and I developed an instant rapport, as though we were brothers, and Patricia-Rochelle impressed me as one of the most dynamic women in the New Age movement.

Earlier that year, she had been doing a reading for a healer in California when one of the subject's future lives had come through. Patricia-Rochelle ("PRD" to her friends) had been able to perceive that the healer would experience a future incarnation as a medical doctor, and amazingly, that physician from tomorrow was in the process of channeling future knowledge through the healer.

"Think of it, Brad," she said excitedly. "If we begin to tap into our future lives, we will be able to bring back talents, knowledge, skills, and abilities—and use them now!"

In November of 1973, PRD made contact with her own future self, Orion (Or-E-on), who would be born in Honolulu in 2832. Such a projection on the moebius strip of time had completed a kind of trinity for her. Earlier, she had gained awareness of a prior existence as a light being who had come to this planet in a time capsule from Ursa Major 660,000 years ago. She had come to understand that her present life experience was a blending of the incarnations in between, plus a composite of the 35,000 men and women for whom she had done consultations. Now she had added the future perspective of the entity Orion.

On February 9, 1974, on Patricia-Rochelle's fiftieth birthday, Orion came through PRD in an incredible burst of cosmic energy.

"She channeled for about an hour and a half," Jon informed me. "But we have over three hours of Orion's messages on tape. Somehow he managed to stretch time!"

It has now become common for PRD to move out of the way and permit Orion to come through. From his unique vantage point in the future flow of time, he is able to channel wisdom of an intensely practical nature.

"Yes," Patricia-Rochelle agreed with a warm smile of confirmation. "We can begin right now to evolve into our future selves. We can speed up our present life experience and live through more than one life at a time. Such a process will bring increased knowledge into the present life and grant a greater reality than before.

I have taught the process to several scientists and inventors who are now bringing back certain aspects of their future work into today.

During consultations, Patricia-Rochelle has been able to assist people in unlocking their own doors to higher consciousness and permitting them to release old karmic hangups so that they might move into more productive lives.

I asked her to itemize the factors that she considered to be immediate benefits of future life knowledge. Among the items she listed were:

1. The ability to identify your soul mission;
2. The ability to evaluate what your potential was at birth;
3. The awareness to recognize major karmic problems and to solve them now;
4. The power to release negative programming;
5. The knowledge to assess your current potential;
6. The ability to establish your future potential.

Orion has channeled through Patricia-Rochelle "The Nine Divisions of Time as Related to Existence in Form." According to this wise being from the future, it is well to be guided through these divisions of time in order to be able to reach the most powerful aspects of the future self.

"In order to more productively build the awareness of one's future existence," Patricia-Rochelle was told, "one must first retrace some old territory. Once those footsteps have again become familiar, the psyche is ready to soar, unfettered, into the future."

As a serious researcher, I have found it extremely useful to direct my subject's through Orion's "Nine Divisions of Time." Fellow researchers, as well as seekers of awareness and advanced students of metaphysics, may profit immeasurably from such journeys.

The Past/Past: In an altered state of consciousness (ASC) you can move back to explore the unrecorded history of this planet or any other planet. You can find the true origin of your soul. You can travel in the psyche to other worlds and other universes.

The Past/Present: This area of time constitutes the memories of past lives in recorded Earth history.

The Past/Future: An examination of this facet of time can help you understand how happenings from the past may be affecting your present life.

The Present/Past: This is the moment just before your conception, the cosmic tick of Time when your soul made the decision to enter the particular body of the present life with its environmental situations and its future potentials.

The Present/Past: Esoterically, the Now is the time/space that existed since four and one-half days ago and the four and one-half days that will happen from the Now.

The Present/Future: This is from the Now to the end of one's present incarnation. During the process of being guided through this aspect of time, you can begin to understand how your years may be stretched into a longer life if you decide to follow the evolutionary path and the cosmic laws that govern the Universe.

The Future/Past: In an ASC, it is most beneficial to view your next incarnation from the perspective of the present-life experience. You will be able to perceive that you create your own future reality and begin to lay down the pattern for your future life by the deeds of the present.

The Future/Present: You are able, while in a deep altered state, to be brought to a heightened awareness that permits you to draw knowledge, wisdom, and love from all of the future incarnations except for the final one. Potentials for the future lives have been created in the lives prior to them, so it is possible for you to be brought to the vantage point where you can make use of talents and abilities from the widest possible spectrum of life experiences.

The Future/Future: The final incarnation brings about total awareness and produces the ultimate human experience. Although these patterns are constantly changing and evolving as you move forward and evolve spiritually, certain meditations and guided visualizations can permit you to gain access to your future self on at least a temporary basis. Although you may not be able to live every moment on the physical plane as the epitome of the complete and fully functioning human, even a glimpse of such perfection may be enough to provide profound inspiration in your present life.

Techniques and Exercises

A young woman we will call Marty had attended several of my lectures over a four or five-year period, but she had a block against entering any kind of altered state of consciousness that would have permitted her to explore either a past or future life. I explained to Marty that much of everyone's normal day is actually spent in an altered state of consciousness and that it is truly natural to enter a trance/dream state. When I had explained my techniques, Marty was willing—and able—as you will be.

The following exercises in creative visualization should help you in your own exploration of your future lives. They have been tested at unnumerable seminars throughout the world, and they have enabled many serious students to obtain meaningful contact with a future aspect of themselves.

You may engage the assistance of a trusted friend or family member to read the relaxation technique and the visualization suggestions to you. Or you may record the instructions in your own voice prior to the experiments.

I recommend that you play some restful, relaxing music to aid you in drifting into an altered state of consciousness. The music you choose should not be a popular melody with a refrain, nor should it contain any vocals. Instrumentals with nonassociative emotional responses will be best. You may even use the soundtrack to such motion picures as *Somewhere in Time, Star Trek,* or *Close Encounters of the Third Kind.* The New Age music of such composers as Steven Halpern, Michael Stearn, or Iasos is strongly recommended.

You may sit or lie down, whichever position is the most comfortable for you. Be certain that your legs and arms remain uncrossed, however, so that you do not shut off normal circulation during the experience.

It is important that you are in a place where you will not be disturbed for at least a half-an-hour. Shut off the telephone or put on the answering machine and go into a room where you cannot hear its shrill and demanding ringing.

Remember always that you are a creator. What you think, you create on some level of consciousness, on some vibratory plane. Where your attention is, there you are. What you wish, you become. What you meditate upon, you will be.

Before you begin any of the experiments that follow, take a moment to sit quietly. Take a comfortably deep breath; hold it for a slow count of three. Exhale, counting again to three. Repeat this process three times.

Now impress upon all levels of your consciousness that you wish to view scenes from the future that will be for your good and your gaining.

Impress upon all levels of your consciousness, all levels of your awareness, that you wish to view your future potentials.

Impress upon all levels of your consciousness, all levels of your awareness, all aspects of your soul, that you wish to be one with your future self.

Be prepared at this time to let your body relax completely. Permit every muscle to relax. Let your mind begin to drift and to float, then allow yourself to go totally with the relaxation technique. Go as deep within an altered state of consciousness as you can.

It is most important that you do as instructed above. You must follow these instructions if you truly desire to view a future-life experience. That is why it is necessary that you choose a time and a place when and where you will not be disturbed.

None of the exercises in this chapter should be attempted until you or your subject is in as relaxed a state as possible. The relaxation technique should be read slowly, in a soft, measured voice. The same measured tone should be utilized in the exercises.

You must permit your body to relax completely so that your mind may begin to soar to the in-between Universe, the one that exists between this world of physical reality and the eternal now, the timeless realm beyond the normal limitations of material time and space. Your mind must be permitted to travel to the eternal now where it can make contact with your future self.

The Nine Golden Steps Technique

Visualize yourself standing before a stairway of golden steps. Understand that these steps will take you into the future. As you proceed toward the future, you will begin to perceive information that you need to know for your good and your gaining.

Step One: Feel every muscle in your body begin to relax. With every breath you take, you find that you are relaxing more and more. With every breath that you take, you find that your senses are becoming keener, your mind clearer.

Step Two: Understand that with each step upward that you take you will be moving closer to the future—closer to the perception of a skill, an ability, a knowledge that you will be able to use in your present life experience.

Step Three: Feel a new energy entering your body. With every breath that you take, you are feeling more focused, more centered.

Step Four: You are aware of a beautiful energy of peace and love entering your consciousness. And with every breath that you take, you are becoming more and more relaxed.

Step Five: Feel a new confidence entering your consciousness. You know that you are a spiritually evolving entity, moving into new awareness, new opportunities for growth and gaining. Feel this understanding permeating your very essence.

Step Six: Know and understand that your new awarenesses will always take you into the future to perceive and to comprehend tomorrow in a way that will serve the Oneness and the Light. Know and understand that you have the ability to perceive the future and to transform the energy of tomorrow into a new and more creative reality today.

Step Seven: With every breath you take, you are becoming more relaxed, more at peace, more at one with the blessed Harmony that governs the Universe. You know that you have the ability—if it is to be for your good and your gaining—to perceive that facet of the future about which you need to know.

Step Eight: Know and understand that the challenges of tomorrow can also enrich the wisdom of today. Know and understand that you have the ability to perceive what you need to know to help you build a more positive present, to construct a more harmonious today. Know and understand that when you step up to Number Nine, you will be able to see yourself in a future life. You will be able to see yourself doing something, performing some activity, or interacting with materials that will have meaning for the tasks of today. You will be able to know and to understand what it is that you are doing. You will know and understand how you will be able to transform this new knowledge, this new skill, this new ability into a practical application for today. You will know and understand all these things when you step up to Number Nine.

Step Nine: See before you now the wonderful Golden Step Number Nine. You know and understand that you will only see that which you need to see for your good and for your gaining and for your present-life enrichment.

Step up to Golden Number Nine. See before you now that which it is that you are to perceive for your good, your gaining, and your present life enrichment. You will know and understand precisely what it is that you are perceiving and how you are to transform it into positive productivity and life enrichment—today.

You will return to full consciousness whenever you wish.

The Relaxation Technique

Imagine yourself sitting or lying down in your favorite place. Perhaps you are lying on a blanket on a beautiful stretch of beach. Or you may be leaning against a sturdy oak tree near a quietly bubbling stream. Or you may be traveling back in your memory to a secret place that you enjoyed when you were a child—a secret place where you retreated when the world closed in on you.

Wherever this favorite place may be, you are seeing yourself there now. You are feeling very comfortable, very relaxed. With every breath that you take, you are finding yourself becoming more and more relaxed.

As you relax, you know that nothing will disturb you. Nothing will distress you in any way. Nothing will molest you or bother you.

You know that you have nothing to fear. You are aware of the presence of your guide, and you know that you are surrounded by the essence of love from the very heart of the Universe.

Nothing can harm you. As you begin to relax more and more, you will feel all tensions, all fears, all anxieties leaving your body. Every muscle is relaxing; every part of your body is relaxing.

With every breath you take, you find yourself feeling more relaxed. With every breath you take, you find yourself feeling better and better. With every breath you take, you feel love moving around you like a gentle, warm breeze.

You know that you must permit your body to relax so that you may rise to higher states of awareness. Your body must relax so that the real you may rise higher and higher to greater levels of understanding.

You are feeling the beautiful energy of tranquility, peace, and love entering your body; and now you are especially aware of this loving energy entering your feet. You feel every muscle in your feet relaxing, every muscle in your feet being soothed and calmed.

The beautiful energy of tranquility, peace, and love moves up your legs into your ankles, your calves, your knees, your thighs; and you feel every muscle in your ankles, your calves, your knees, and your thighs relaxing, relaxing, feeling soothed and calmed.

Nothing will disturb you. Nothing will distress you in any way. If you should hear any sound at all—a slamming door, a honking horn, a shouting voice—that sound will not disturb you. That sound will help you to relax even more.

Now the beautiful energy of tranquility, peace, and love is moving into your hips, your stomach, your back; and you feel every muscle in your hips, your stomach, your back relaxing, relaxing, relaxing.

With every breath you take, you find that your body is becoming more and more relaxed. Your mind is becoming clearer and more focused. You know that you have the ability to explore a future lifetime. You know that you have the ability to explore a future life experience for your good and your gaining.

The beautiful energy of tranquility, peace, and love enters your chest, your shoulders, your arms, your fingers; and you feel every muscle in your chest, your shoulders, your arms, and your fingers relaxing, relaxing, relaxing.

With every breath that you take, you find that you are becoming more and more relaxed. Every part of your body is becoming free of tensions, free of worry, free of fear.

The beautiful energy of tranquility, peace, and love moves into your neck, your face, and the very top of your head, relaxing you, relaxing you, relaxing you.

Your body is now completely relaxed, but your mind, your true self, is very much aware and very ready to explore a future lifetime.

You have nothing to fear. Your guide is with you. You are surrounded by love from the very heart of the Universe.

As you move into a future-life experience, you will be able to study it and analyze it without experiencing any tension, fear, or discomfort. Should you at any time see anything that disturbs you or causes you any fear or tension, you have the ability to awaken immediately.

And now the purple mist of time is moving around you, swirling around you. You have the ability to move into future tense, to exist in a future-life experience. You have the ability to remember clearly all that you need to remember for your good and your gaining.

You feel the presence of your guide, and you know that nothing can harm you. You feel love moving all around you.

At the count of three, you will step through the purple mist of time and see yourself in a future time.

One. . .scenes are becoming clearer. *Two*. . .clearer still. Images are beginning to form before your eyes. *Three*. . .you are there in the future.

The Museum of the Future Exercises

Visualize yourself walking through a great and magnificent museum in some future dimension of being. This museum is dedicated to men and women of accomplishment, and it depicts these individuals in holographic, three-dimensional representations.

As you turn the corner, you suddenly find yourself face-to-face with a portrait of an individual that you know is you in a future-life experience. Even though the figure may not greatly resemble you in your present-life experience, you are certain beyond all doubt that it is you.

Take careful notice of various aspects of the holographic representation.

Is the figure male or female?

How large is the figure?

What color is the figure's hair and in what style is it worn?

How is the figure dressed?

In what pose has the holographic picture been fashioned?

What is the figure doing?

From what you can assume, in what field of thought, endeavor, or accomplishment will you excel?

Study the representation carefully. Feel yourself becoming one with the portrait. Feel yourself breathing life and warmth into the hologram. See yourself living the important events of that future lifetime that will result in your representation in this great museum of tomorrow.

In what country or place will you live?

What will be your greatest ambition in that lifetime? What will you want most to accomplish?

See yourself struggling toward your goal in that future life experience. See if you sense or perceive anyone from your present-life experience who may be working with you in that future lifetime. If you recognize anyone at all, take a few moments to contemplate what lesson was left unlearned in your present lifetime that has brought you together with that individual in your future-life experience.

Scan that future lifetime and visualize the events of greatest conflict. See if you sense or perceive anyone from your present life striving against you in that future time. If you recognize anyone at all, take a few moments to contemplate what lesson was left unlearned in your present lifetime that has brought you together with that individual in your future-life experience.

For your good and your gaining, know and understand if you will achieve your goal in that future-life experience.

What will be the most important lesson that you will learn from that lifetime?

What talents or abilities from that future time would you most like to bring back to your present life experience?

See clearly your special talents and gifts in that time, and now understand that you have the ability to bring these skills and accomplishments back with you and to use them productively in your present life.

At the count of five, you will find yourself fully awake, feeling very, very good in mind, body and spirit. *One*. . .coming awake. *Two* . . . coming awake feeling very good. Better than you have felt in weeks and weeks, months and months. *Three* . . . coming awake filled with the talents and abilities of that future lifetime. *Four* . . . coming awake, knowing that you have the power and the ability to use whatever talents you wish from that future time. *Five* . . . coming wide awake, filled with love, wisdom, and knowledge.

A Quest for Future-Life Visions

After you or your subject has been placed in a state of relaxation, reverie, and receptivity, say. . .

See yourself walking along a peaceful beach at night. You can hear the soothing, rhythmic roll of the ocean. You pause in your walk to listen to the sound of the waves gently touching the shore.

Imagine yourself sitting down to relax. You gaze up at the night sky, splashed with a million stars. You can see the sky from horizon to horizon. You feel in harmony with Earth and sky.

As you look up at the night sky, you begin to notice a particularly brilliant, flashing star high overhead. As you watch it, it begins to move toward you. It lowers through the air toward you.

Now you see that it is not a star at all. It is a beautifully glowing object. You feel no fear, only expectation. You feel secure in the love of the Universe. You know that your guide is near you. You feel unconditional love as the object with the sparkling, swirling lights settles near you. Your inner awareness tells you that it is a vehicle that has come to take you to the future. Your inner knowing tells you that this is a time machine that will permit you to glimpse aspects of future lives you need to know about for your good and for your gaining.

A door is opening in the side of the light vehicle. You look inside and see that it is lined with plush, soft purple velvet. You see that the interior of the craft is glowing with the golden light of protection, the light of unconditional love from the very heart of the Universe.

Step inside and settle back against the soft, comfortable cushions. The door silently closes, and you know that the time machine will take you to the eternal now, wherein past, present, and future dwell as one. You are completely comfortable, relaxed, soothed.

You feel pure, unconditional love all around you as you rise to higher dimensions of reality. You are being taken to a vibration of a finer, more highly realized awareness. You know that you are safe. You know that some benevolent force is taking you to the timeless realm. You know that you will be granted meaningful visions of the future when you reach the eternal now.

And now your light vehicle has come to a stop. You look out a window and see that you have stopped before a great, gigantic crystal that seems to be suspended in space.

You are aware in your inner knowing that when you gaze into that great crystal, you will be able to receive and to comprehend meaningful visions of the future. You will be able to receive visions that have been designed especially for you, designed to provide you with deep and profound insights and understandings.

As you gaze into a facet of the great crystal suspended in space, you are beginning to receive images of your first vision of the future.

The first vision appears before you, sent by the Source of All That Is. The first vision shows you scenes from a future life of great accomplishment.

You see clearly whether you are a male or a female. You see how you are dressed, your height, general body size, the color of your hair.

You see yourself performing a particular task for which you will be very well known. See what you are holding in your hands.See clearly what it is that you are doing. See clearly your environment, your surroundings.

See yourself receiving high praise for a special accomplishment. See and know clearly for your good and your gaining how it was that you achieved such an honor. Know and understand how your accomplishment benefits humankind.

Know and understand how certain skills in your present life experience have evolved to these accomplishments of the future. See clearly how you might establish a stronger link to your future life of great accomplishment.

Now your second vision of the future is beginning to manifest. This vision, sent to your awareness by the Source of All That Is, shows you scenes from a future life of unusual abilities.

You see clearly whether you are a male or a female. You see what you are wearing, your height, your general body size, the color of your hair. You also see where you are living as you would understand it in your present life experience.

This is a future life in which you manifest remarkable abilities of telepathy, precognition, clairvoyance, and other gifts of the mind and spirit. This is a lifetime in which you are able to develop freely those abilities that are repressed by society in your present-life experience.

See yourself manifesting a particular aspect of mind power for which you will become especially known. See clearly what it is that you are doing. Be aware of the energy that flows through you. Notice the faces and sense the emotions of those who observe you.

Be aware of the mind set that enables you to make use of this power of the spirit. Know and understand how you use this ability to benefit humankind.

Look at the eyes of those around you. See if any of those men or women have come with you from your present-life experience. Be aware of anyone who has come with you in this future life experience to complete a lesson left unlearned, to complete a work left undone.

Know and understand how certain aspects and abilities of your present-life experience have evolved to these accomplishments and mental manifestations of the future. See clearly how you might establish a stronger link to your future life of unusual abilities.

Now your third vision of the future is beginning to manifest. Your third vision, sent to you by the Source of All That Is, explains to you the past-life experience that was most important to your future evolution.

This is the past-life experience that has been the most influential in achieving dramatic Soul growth. This is the life of sowing for which you will one day reap great spiritual rewards. You will now be shown—and you will understand—the importance of this previous life experience in terms of your soul's evolution of the Source of All That Is.

You will see details of that past life that will help you to understand your present life and that will allow you to observe the path of spiritual evolution you will follow to the future. You will see details that will help you to understand the way you are now and will permit you to chart your path of greater awareness that moves to a future life experience.

You will see for your good and for your gaining the interaction of karma as it blends past, present, and future.

You will see clearly who has come with you from past lives to the present—and who will come with you to the future.

Your fourth vision of the future sent to you from the Source of All That Is is showing you the face of the Earth in the new age.

You are seeing the face of this planet as it will look after any Earth changes have fully taken place. You are being shown changes in society . . . art . . . politics . . . economics . . . clothing styles.

But most important you are being shown the skylines of cities, the definition of coastal regions. You will not be shocked or disturbed by anything that you may see.

You will not be distressed if new coastlines have been formed . . . if new mountain ranges have appeared . . . if cities have gone underground. You will not be disturbed even if alien species should now walk among us. You will see, and you will understand. You will see clearly and understand for your good and for your gaining.

And now from the vantage point of looking backward from the future, you will see where the safe places will be for you. See clearly a map of the United States . . . Canada . . . the world—wherever you wish. For your good and your gaining, the safe places for you will glow with a golden energy. You have the ability to see and to understand where the safe places will be for you.

And now your space vehicle, your time machine, is once again beginning to move. It will now take you back to Earth time, back to human time, back to present time, back to your present life experience.

You will remember all that you have seen of the future that will be for your good and your gaining. The memory of the future will strengthen you to face the challenges and the learning experiences of your present life. You know that you have the ability to bring back from the future all those talents, skills, and accomplishments that can benefit your present life experience.

You are now awakening, surrounded by light and by love. You are coming awake enveloped by pure, unconditional love.

You feel very, very good in mind, body, and spirit. You feel better than you have felt in weeks and weeks, months and months, years and years.

You will awaken fully at the count of *five*.

Conclusion

The exercises given here can help you slip into the future and return bearing treasures. You can renew your confidence in yourself by seeing a future triumph or achievement. You can discover the skills and techniques you'll use in a future lifetime, and bring them back to enrich your life now. You can release the hidden potential in yourself when you see how your talents will be used—and appreciated by others—in a future life. You can do all this for your good and your gaining.

4 Huna: Key to the Mystery of Life

by Enid Hoffman

Huna means "secret" in Hawaiian. A psycho-religious system with its roots in antiquity, Huna was introduced into the United States in the 1930s by Max Freedom Long. Its Hawaiian practitioners, called *Kahunas,* are known for working "miracles" by using their psychic abilities. This ancient tradition offers a model of the Universe that explains many of life's greatest mysteries.

The Huna worldview proposes that we live in two worlds, so intertwined that they appear as one. A symbol of this premise could be two colors spinning in the same space, quite different in hue and tone, but appearing to be one. When spinning slowly enough, both colors can be seen, but when speeded up an illusion of another one is created. What appears to be purple, for example, may actually be red and blue spinning so fast in the same space that they create a "relationship" image of a third color.

I call these two worlds, for convenience, the world of "mental matter," from its densest object formation to its most subtle detectable energy, and the world of "conscious substance," invisible, undetectable, unchanging consciousness itself. Consciousness, as I use the term, is the matrix of our Universe of matter in all its myriad forms.

In the Huna model of a human being, each of us consists of three "selves" whose purpose is to serve the *monad* within. The high self or *Aumakua* serves by creating the dramas of dreams, the low self or *Unihipili* by maintaining the physical body and all its functions, and the middle self or *Uhane* by thinking, conceptualizing, organizing and expressing the monad's will and feeling. We can think of these three selves as the Divine self (Aumakua), the human self (Uhane) and the animal self (Unihipili). One of our goals in life, according to the Huna belief system, is to establish good communication between the three selves so that they work together effectively as a "team."

The techniques, exercises, and meditations included in this chapter are designed to help us shift our understanding and comprehension into a context within which we can "wake up" to our innate powers of awareness. Gradually we can move into a position of control over our own personal minds. New relationships open up between us and our three selves. Following that, new internal relationships within our minds can change our lifestyles radically, preparing us for more productive future lives of cooperation between the infinite and the finite. By working with Huna we can create the lifetimes we desire to live, now and in the future.

The Monad

Monads are units of substantial consciousness. By using the word "monad" for you and me, I can keep away from the many confusing descriptions of the "self." I can distinguish more clearly between the ego identity and the real, authentic center of a human being. An aware monad has no center of its own, but it is free to center within a human being (or any other mental form) and to go in and out of a physical body periodically and cyclically. A monad may enter into a physical form for a cycle known as a finite lifetime. The beginning of this cycle is the birth of an infant, the end of the cycle is called physical death. To my knowledge, one lifetime is the longest cycle a monad may undertake in physical form. This planet's daily cycle of approximately twenty-four hours is the shortest cycle. During a twenty-four-hour cycle, a monad has the opportunity to separate from the mind during deep sleep and return "home" to its consciousness.

Huna proposes that it is consciousness that gives all finite things their meaning and purpose. The growth and expansion of awareness in each monadic unit is the purpose of all forms. To serve consciousness, rather than having consciousness serve the mind, is the goal of living the Huna way.

Consciousness is here and now, always, inpacting on the where and when of every separate form. Consciousness is the source of all actuality. The greatest illusion is to believe that the physical world is the source of consciousness, and that within the mind, there is the power to create and dominate consciousness itself!

Each of us has lived many lives previous to this one and will live out many more finite lives in the future. In order to exercise some choice of what our potential lives can be, we need to know exactly "who" you and I are. Each of us is a human being, and each human being is both monad and mind—two very personal worlds of experience. It is the monad that is eternal, infinite and which continues after the death of the physical vehicle.

Throughout history the aware/conscious being has been given many names. Monad is one name. The Italian philosopher Bruno Giordano (1548?—1600) coined the word "monad" and developed the philosophy of monadism. He pictured the world as being composed of *individual elements of conscious being.* Ultimate and irreducible, manifest in every person and in all other living creatures, monads are the units of conscious substance which are the essence of being. These ultimate constituents are immaterial and possess the capacity of awareness (perception and direct cognition). Giordano developed the theory that only rational monads have "apperception" or the ability to be aware of their own minds and mental parts as separate from consciousness. He was burned to death as a heretic. This conscious/awareness substance, the essence of being human, is what a monad is. It is unextended, indivisible, unobstructed and impenetrable. Monadic conscious substance is the matrix of the mind, whether universal or personal. As in the macrocosm, so in the microcosm.

The Three Selves

You, as a monad, are the central axis around which your personal world revolves. Each of us is an individual monad who has at least three divisions of mind with which we work to create our actual life experiences. In Huna, we call these three divisions "selves." These selves function simultaneously, and each holds one aspect of mentality.

In the Hawaiian tradition the three selves were also called "spirits," independent of each other, separate but interacting functional selves. Spirit is defined as the essential nature of an idea. As the three are discussed further you will be able to recognize their actuality in your own experiences. Each of these three selves is composed of many parts.

Unihipili is a nature spirit with an elemental mind. In another culture, Unihipili might be called a Deva. It is in charge of all the elemental intelligences that belong to the "lower kingdoms" that produce and maintain our physical world: the spirits of minerals, vegetables, and all living creatures.

Unihipili manifests and actualizes your physical-etheric body. You create your own physical-etheric body according to what you choose or allow your ego to decide. For example, if you decide to be healthy, you create a healthy body. Unihipili is said to be centered in the solar plexus, so when relating to it, you can focus your attention on that place in your body. It is easy to communicate to your Unihipili, for it is receptive to every word (literally), every image in your mind, and every thought! From all these things, Unihipili culls the forms that make up your physical existence.

The most dense subtle body is Unihipili's etheric one. The next body, less dense than the etheric, belongs to the middle self, *Uhane;* it often is called the astral body. You may think of Uhane as your "conscious self" or "day self," active and reactive during the day, resting at night. Sometimes, however, Uhane worries, fears and is apprehensive. At such times, it can be reluctant to let you leave for your nightly release.

Uhane holds your public identity, social status and self esteem. All thought forms of who and what you are, all the concepts and beliefs that people have developed through historical time are contained in your Uhane. Unihipili holds your racial and genetic characteristics, and Uhane holds the social concepts about those.

Most monads live so fully encased in the Uhane thought form that they are nearly out of touch with Unihipili, and with *Aumakua,* the highest self or spirit each monad has. Aumakua is a spirit-idea which I call "the genius." Like the genie trapped in a bottle, most of our geniuses are unavailable to us. When we are trapped with in our ego identity, we cannot develop a relationship with this higher self except through dreams. Dreams are the medium by which Aumakua helps us, "speaking" to us from the mental plane it inhabits.

Each of us has a genius, a private tutor and guide who guards us and teaches us by drawing us toward those experiences we are ready for. When you are willing to encounter something and able to cope with it, your genius will present it for you. Socrates had his "daemon," da Vinci displayed his genius in his art and scientific creations. So have many others whom we call "geniuses." You have your own unique personal genius working with you, but before you can utilize its potential you must do the ground work that gets you "ready."

Thought Forms

Think of each self as a living thought form with a central idea (or spirit). Every thought form body is an energy field, revolving around a central idea or spirit. The spiritual energy keeps the field in motion and coherent, with boundaries. Every thought must have an idea-spirit and a boundary. Once the spirit loses meaning and purpose for existence, it dissolves like a cloud.

Thought forms are born, persist as a process and then end; they dissolve, disappear or die. So all selves are born, live and die.

To persist, a thought form must be enspirited with an idea. Each monad produces many ideas which create many thought forms. The physical body is one such thought form. Unihipili is the idea spirit of the human animal. Each of us has a somatic thought form that holds our personal concepts about our physical lives and bodies. This thought form exists as a background to the physical or "dense" body, and has been called the etheric body. At the center of some thought forms you will find a monad. At the center of others you may find an idea or "spirit" of that form. History, for example, is a component of mind, and being the "content" of mind it takes shape as a collection of thought forms. As you, the monad, read this, your mental processes are ingesting and digesting this in accordance with the mentally-constructed bodies you currently have functioning.

Linear time—past, present and future—belongs to the mind. The concept of time, personal or universal, past or future, is a thought form created by the mind, shaped and formed by the mind. All future existences presently energized by the mind, actually are past possessions. The moment of existence, the moment of creation, becomes past in the mental world.

Once we are able to accept that we create, individually and jointly with others in our societies, everything that we experience in our world—past, present and future—we can set about creating the thought forms we desire with aware intent, rather than haphazardly. In doing so, we will take charge of our futures—in this physical existence and in future lifetimes in other bodies.

Memory

Unihipili holds all actual memories of physical experiences, whether the monad was in or out of the body at the time. (When there is physical trauma, many monads choose to go out of the body for a bit, returning when the trauma is lessened. Special techniques must be used to tap these memories.)

Uhane's mind holds a certain class of memories: the concepts, abstract ideas, paradigms and models of the world, and all of its conscious and pre-conscious events. All our social stereotypes as well as all ego structures reside in the mind and memory of Uhane.

Aumakua's memory bank is ancestral, holding all the archetypes created by societies and cultures. All contents of all cultural geniuses are there, too, ready to be tapped by monads that are ready, willing and able to utilize this knowledge. All the conceptual gods and goddesses of all time live in archetypal splendor here.

Sometimes a monad will create a thought form before the time is right for it to manifest in actuality. The outcome is held as a *seed thought,* to come into being at some other time, when conditions are appropriate. The monad creates the thought form in complete detail and places it in a thin, lovely shell to protect it for the future. This is what I meant in my earlier statement that all future existences actually are past possessions; the "future" has already been created—though this does not mean that it cannot be changed. It can—by creating new thought forms and seed thoughts that will be released and grow in the future. For instance, you may have already stored away a seed thought that will result in career success at some future time, when you feel and believe you are ready to experience it. Or, you may have created the seed thought that later on will manifest as cancer if you allow it to come into fruition. Many minds in unison create the seed thoughts for the future of the world: peace and prosperity, or war and destruction.

Creating Your Future

Many of us let our current minds make decisions for us, rather than choosing with awareness and intent what we want. Too often we allow our minds to dominate us, behaving like unruly children. We let ourselves be dominated by the selves that should be serving us! The first task, therefore, is to transform the relationships we have with each of them. Uhane is there to act out and express exactly and truly what we choose to express; Unihipili provides the ability and the energy to act it out, to do the appropriate thing, elegantly and excellently. We must choose to be both willing and willful, taking responsibility for all our selves as our products. We must think of them as our "helpers," whom we direct.

You have a wonderful team that you can motivate to accomplish all your goals. Once they are in accord with you, the monad, all they need is to be clearly shown the outcomes you want them to accomplish.

Using a Pendulum

Here is a technique you can use to begin creating the future self you desire. You may want to choose a future "where" or "when"; however, these details are often most wisely decided by your Aumakua. If you do decide to make those choices, I suggest you ask your Aumakua for inspiration and guidance.

Begin by teaching your Unihipili to swing a pendulum for the purpose of removing any barriers that may exist to creating the future self you really want. Your Unihipili has access to all memories, all beliefs, all attitudes that are related to your life now and in the future. Sometimes there are attitudes or concepts that must be cleared away so that your path to that future is free and easy. Any parts of your mind or selves that are not in accord with the new model of yourself and your life in the future need to be revised or dissolved.

You can purchase a pendulum or make one by fixing an object about the size and weight of a nickle at the end of three-to-four inches of cord or chain. Hold the cord between your thumb and forefinger above a table or desk top. You may rest your elbow on the surface if it's more comfortable for you.

Tell Unihipili to swing the pendulum back and forth in front of you for "yes" and sideways for "no." Then begin your questioning. Ask first for the categories within which barriers reside: beliefs, attitudes, attachments, ideas, fears, etc. After determining no or yes for each category, decide which category you should tackle first. Ask Unihipili for a numerical rating of each category on the list, or ask which is the most important if your list contains at least ten.

As you continue, Unihipili will become convinced you really want to know, and therefore, more material that is relevant to the task will rise into your awareness. Emphasize your willingness to know the barriers and your will to achieve the goal of creating a new future self.

You now can recognize yourself as a conscious monad and the parent of all your "offspring." This allows you to become the observer, a dispassionate creator who is neither to be blamed nor praised for the personality existing, but who is totally responsible for the conditions and situations that you experience.

Communicating with Uhane

Your next task is to use a technique which will enable you to experience a small gap between you and your mind, to step out, momentarily, in imagination from your mind. This technique is also extremely helpful for the would-be meditator who is "harassed" by thoughts and ideas when attempting to be quiet.

Begin by relaxing your physical body. Show your intention to relax by firmly stating that you wish it to happen, now. Next focus your attention on each part of your physical body in turn. Begin with your breath, and order your breathing to slow and deepen, to become regular and easy. Next you may go to either your feet or the top of your head, whichever you prefer and focus your attention on successive body parts as you direct them to relax. Experience them fully in relaxing. When the body is relaxed, silently thank your Unihipili. (Note: You may choose to call your Unihipili by a particular name, and to refer to it by that name during these exercises.)

Next, convey to your Uhane that you are going to listen carefully to whatever message it may want to present to you. The procedure for doing this is new, and you will need to make the process clear to your Uhane. Advise your Uhane that all thoughts and communications from it must enter your awareness one at a time from the left, proceed across and in front of your head, and exit to the right. Tell your Uhane that you will observe very carefully all communications it desires to make at this time.

Throughout this procedure, remain uninvolved, detached and unconcerned about any of the information that flows across your awareness. The data must arise into your awareness, then keep moving in a serene, continuous, flowing motion. Just watch, as you would a movie. Observe it carefully and respectfully. If at any moment your body comes out of its state of total relaxation, start again.

Remember to keep your journal and a pen or pencil handy during this exercise so you can make notes of this first experiment. If your Uhane reminds you of something important, pause, write it down, and then continue. The objective is to allow Uhane to empty its mind of everything it wants to communicate to you. As the flow slows, encourage Uhane to empty itself fully before it relaxes and becomes quiet. Uhane will grow calm when it realizes that both you and it are safe, and you are in command of the personality.

This experience will create the space you need to be creative. This is an important step in transfering authority over your life into your keeping. That gap between you and the contents of your mind will allow you to perceive that your thoughts are not YOU, and therefore they are under your control. No beliefs, no attitudes, no content of any kind has any genuine power over you anymore.

Finishing Your Unfinished Business

In order to develop new relationships with your selves and their parts, it is necessary to use the technique of *Naming and Framing*. This technique is ancient, but its meaning and significance have been lost in many cultures. Polynesian peoples have retained knowledge of it and Huna masters use it skillfully to "call out" or "call up" any thought form needed to bring about transformation or change.

Once you are familiar and comfortable with Unihipili, Uhane and Aumakua, you can begin to get to know all the sub-selves that exist within your three "major" selves. There is magic in "naming and framing" any part of your mind to give it "spirit" or focus within a framework of concepts "about" it. Each "thought form" enspirited, thus, can be known by direct cognition.

Most of us have internalized parents, guardians, protectors and critics galore. Each of these becomes a sub-self to the major three. These mental units make most of our decisions, control our physical states, and run our lives totally. As children, when life became painful, we "opted out" frequently, even went out of our bodies when life got very difficult. Every event we cannot remember or did not participate in became "stuck" in linear time as an independent *Event Self* or persisting thought form. These event selves are splinters of you that often inhibit your growth and development. Use ingenuity in naming these selves as you frame them in the event in which they got stuck. By naming them, you can begin to know them and confront them, understand their purpose in your life, and convince them to relax their stranglehold on you so you can move forward toward the future you want.

Because we are such strangers to some of our selves, the next techniques are designed to help us get to know them better, recall their "unfinished business" into awareness, and gather up all the "stuck parts" so as to heal and integrate their energy into the self-system.

Begin by appreciating all that your mind, in its separate selves, has done to keep you here in the body, alive and learning. Start with a few simple "thank yous." Here is where your will to know your own mind must become firm and determined. If there is any part that repels you, that you loathe, that you would rather not know, then you will not meet it, be assured. Until you totally accept all of your selves, you will find they can easily escape your awareness.

Start by listing every emotion that perturbs, agitates or excites your mind. Worry, fear, anger, irritation and hate are a few. All these emotions exist as past mind parts, created historically and moving into the future through the present, whenever they are triggered by events.

For example, I call the worrier in me "Worry Wart." (She handles all my fears, too.) "Melancholy Me" covers self-pity. "Peter Pan" is the part of me that refuses to become an adult. "Wendy" is the part that feels obliged to worry about other people and to take care of them as if they were helpless or stupid. This part is a cultural "mother" who "cares" by fearing for. "Pack Rat" is the name I choose for my sub-self who tries to alleviate my insecurity by collecting things and possessions, and storing them even when I do not need them, creating meaningless attachments. You are welcome to use these names for your own sub-selves. Add to the list, too. If we can come to know ALL our selves and integrate them, transforming stuck energy into fluid energy, we will become stronger, more vital, more creative and more ALIVE.

Now relax your physical body and your mind, and when all selves are serene, instruct them to perform for you while you observe. They are going to project out in front of you, in imagination, as though on a movie screen, each mind-part you name. They are going to help you "set the scene" for this projection, and it will be one you will use over and over, many times. Read the following carefully—you may even wish to record it on tape so you can play it back to yourself at other times.

To your left is a lovely meadow. The sun is shining in a very blue sky and a few white, puffy clouds are floating by. In the meadow, grasses and flowers make a lovely pattern of colors and shapes at your feet. Now smell the scent of grass in the sun and the fragrance of flowers. A breeze touches your skin and you sense the warmth of the sunshine in the breeze; you hear the hum of insects.

On your right it is shady and cool, for trees arch over a brook. Around the brook is deep, dark, moist soil and you can hear gurgling as the stream tumbles down a hill. A breeze blows across the stream toward you, carrying the refreshing scent of moist earth and cool water. The dappled sunshine dances on the ground and around the brook, causing the water to sparkle.

Now see stretching out in front of you a straight path leading to a grove of trees. This grove will be the background for your projections from your selves. As you look toward the trees, instruct silently that one selected sub-self will be projected into that grove of trees.

Now let that sub-self emerge from the wood in a clear and easily perceived form. This form has many features that you observe and note for study later. Every single aspect is full of significance and meaning. As it nears you, keep observing without analyzing or speculating. The form stops near you and you begin a dialogue. Ask its name. Ask questions and you will receive answers, though they may not be conveyed in words. Ideas and thoughts flow from that form to you. Let your own thoughts respond. Let this form know that you are its source, and you desire to know it completely.

Tell this self that you accept it totally as it is and that it need not hide anything from you. You are ready, willing and able to know it fully. You are ready to accept and love it as your own creation. Allow knowledge about this form to flood your awareness. Ask it to show you events and experiences from your past in which it was involved. Let it communicate anything it can to you at this time.

When it feels right to do so, say farewell to this self until next time. Let the form go back into the woods until your mind chooses to retrieve it for another visit at another time. When you call it up the next time, using the same name, you may find this mind-part has changed significantly as a result of your first encounter! In this way, you will achieve integration of all your sub-selves eventually.

After using the first two techniques to change your present life, examine in revery the changes that have resulted from these experiments. Utilize these changes to create new contexts (with your selves) within which you can learn and grow. The next technique is designed to create a future context within which you can further the evolution of your consciousness. This technique enables you to begin creating a future personality which will be an efficient vehicle for you, as a monad, to allow your genius to manifest and contribute to your culture in a meaningful way.

Creating the Ideal You

You hold within you an ego ideal. This is the "ideal person" you have envisioned, according to the cultural concepts that influence you. This ego ideal is a hero or heroine to you—the person you would most like to be. This concept is most meaningful for it reveals what you believe *you are not.*

Begin by listing in your notebook all that you believe you are not. Head pages with sentences that start "I AM NOT..." followed by whatever is appropriate in your beliefs about yourself. Divide the subject into what you think are "desirable" and "undesirable" characteristics for your personality to possess. List all the things you are not and don't want to be, as well as all the things you are not but would love to be in your new personality.

A thought form exists in our minds within that framework of I AM NOT. The creatures we are not are also thought forms with as much validity as the ones that have a spirit or idea of I AM. With the appropriate technique, you can bring into your awareness the thought forms that embrace those characteristics you hold as ego ideals: your heroes and heroines.

After this is done (and it will take awhile) review each page in turn, and then meditate on it. Sit back and close your eyes. Let memories and images arise into your awareness about the events that became contexts for these choices you made. Ask, and keep asking, for understanding of why your choices were most appropriate at that time. That wisdom is within your mind, available to you when you are ready to understand more of your life experiences.

Go over each page to find the self concepts that are derived from something someone said, in speech or writing, about you or to you. We have all been psychically abused through blaming, shaming and humiliation, and these experiences created the selves we believe we cannot be, or refuse to be. We have repressed parts of who we are, but those repressed selves remain with us still. We need only to recognize them, acknowledge and appreciate them to begin integrating them into our "known" selves and utilizing their abilities to our advantage.

By connecting with your beliefs about what you are and what you are not, and by realizing that you have denied many parts of yourself for years because *someone else said you should,* you can begin to eliminate blockages to your goals, your future success and happiness. You can become your own hero or heroine!

Before you can begin creating the future you want, many thought form barriers must be dissolved. All ideas and attitudes that create fear within you should, and can be dissolved. Use the following fantasy to dissolve a thought form of your choosing.

Sit back, relax, then instruct your selves to project out in front of you the form or image of your "fear-full self." State your intent to dissolve it. Think of this solidified fear-energy as a thought form with shape and boundaries. Now see its boundaries melting, blurring, becoming a cloud, and then dispersing into the atmosphere as pure energy. Deal with each fear in turn, until you have dispersed all those fears you've carried around as excess baggage since childhood.

Now you are ready to sow the seeds of your future, by creating the "vehicles" (or bodies) in which you will travel the route from ignorance to wisdom successfully. If you wish the help of higher forces, you will need to abide by a few rules. Your genius will not help unless you are prepared to manifest genius. And genius is only manifest for the benefit of the many, many beings who live on Earth. Genius is not for the satisfaction of individual ego needs or desires. It will not necessarily bring status or social success if those are sought for selfish gratification only. But it does make major contributions to the cultural context within which we all exist.

Unless you are willing to gain new knowledge, you keep repeating experiences from which you have not learned. In order to eliminate repetitious future lives, re-experiencing the same lessons you have not learned, you must establish your willingness to learn from each and every context in which you find yourself. Once you have confirmed your willingness to learn, you need to make certain your foundations are solid and secure.

You must be able to visualize clearly and confidently the future you want for yourself. Then, give those visions of your future lives to your high self, along with your heartfelt feelings, the emotions of your present selves. Follow up this communication with a gift of the life force, a gift of *mana* to enable your higher mind to create an *offspring* which will be a future self for you.

By including service to others as part of your future self, you align yourself with your own genius. Serving others does not mean sacrificing yourself, or suffering and loss for you—quite the opposite. The result of serving is delight and gain.

The image you create will be the etheric body, the blueprint for the physical body of the future, containing all the permanent atoms that have already been collected as permanent intelligence. In each lifetime you experience you accumulate a portion of wisdom, and this manifests as intelligence in the etheric body, which eventually determines the physical body product.

The etheric body is composed of four ethers: light, sound, color and electricity. Waves of light, waves of sound, waves of color and waves of electricity all contribute to their opposite manifestation, particles or parts. We feel the parts as they combine in presence, and we see and hear the waves as sound, light and color.

The etheric vehicle (or body) is transparent, in contrast to the opacity of the physical body. So in your visualizations you'll want to use transparencies, which are great fun in imagination. You can envision layers upon layers of different colors, and see them all!

Certain colors relate to specific qualities, characteristics, attributes, so in order to imbue your future self with the characteristics you desire, you "paint" your etheric vehicle with the appropriate colors.

To select the correct colors and the sounds, use a simple criteria: your own responses to them. How do you feel about them? In imagination you can assign each quality a particular taste and scent to help you separate what is right for you, and what is not. What smells bad or tastes bad, is inappropriate, so let it go. Bring in the lovely fragrant colors and sounds. Bring in the harmonious chords of music and the aesthetically satisfying color combinations.

Give your future self width and depth, containing all the dualities of mind. Visualize the warm, brilliant colors of red, orange and yellow and imagine that they furnish you with all the masculine attributes of leadership, initiative and intellect.

Imagine the deep, clear blues and greens as providing feminine intuition, receptivity and the connection to higher levels of mind that bring into manifestation the actual life form.

Give your thought form boundaries. Begin with a form that is very large, then increasingly apply your own energy force to spin that shape from the future toward the past, so that it may, in time, arrive in some present. See the cloud-like form you have created becoming denser, collapsing in upon itself like any natural process of seed-creation.

In creating that etheric body for a future life, include the qualities of Unihipili, the natural self, the elemental mind, as well as all the qualities of a social being, Uhane. Then include the transpersonal mind, the genius for living—Aumakua—that encompasses the other two and adds a new dimension of experience.

You, the eternal and infinite monad, are always creating future lives. As co-creator with other monads, you create the future societies you will live and learn within. Most of us, however, are not aware of doing so. Awareness is increased by making choices, appropriate and inappropriate, and learning from your choices. Awareness is dulled when you are frightened of "making mistakes," and learning is then limited. By allowing our minds to make decisions based on social criteria we put off making choices, and we become excellent at doing so. Our heritage as monads is free will, or the power that comes with making a choice instead of experiencing events "by default," what we call fate.

Fate overtakes those who are directed and controlled. Destiny is arrived at by controlling and directing a team of selves, selectively shaped and formed with awareness and intent by your choices. Fate is the patterns selected by cultures and societies, the contexts within which the whole consciousness moves as one. Destiny is the pattern created by one individual in order to make a real impact, a cultural improvement on societies at large.

Our future lives are created out of mental matter, now and here. All thoughts about the future become memories that persist. Precipitated out of consciousness, into the world of the mind, enlivened by giving it a "spirit of the future," each thought form pulls us toward it, just like all our expectations do. What ever we imagine we give the power to attract us. Skillful "imaginers" create thought forms with more magnetic force than do people with no knowledge of the process.

Each of us holds internally the patterns of attraction and repulsion, which are designed to work for us in our personal force fields. These fields resonate with the fields of others, creating harmonic or discordant relationships.

Here is where you always are, and now is your time. Your "here" can move to any "where" and your now can "relate" to any of the objective time constructs it wants to. Your "here" can be like a spark of light, darting to and fro, going out of form and wandering the planes of mind, or into levels of consciousness itself. Or your "here," with progression, can become capable of expanding to include vast amounts of universal space while you center in any specific place of your choosing. You and I carry our centers, our places, with us wherever we go. We carry our "now" time also, through the ages, the years, unchanging in nature and essence as a spark of consciousness itself.

Crafting Our 5 Lives through the Cauldron

by Nicki Scully

We are involved in a process of re-awakening, remembering who we are, who we have been, and what our potential for the future is. As we awaken, we are as children discovering all over again our own natures, what skills and talents we possess, and how to apply ourselves to the challenges of this new cycle.

Throughout our awakening process we are assisted by maps and guideposts which are our heritage. Many of these appear in the form of synchronicities: co-incidents tinged with magic. These occurances are quite common. As if by an unseen hand, we are led from place to place, situation to situation, and find ourselves in the presence of just the right person who can help us learn a particular lesson at just the right time. We realize more and more that life is our school and all who come within the sphere of our awareness, physical and non-physical alike, are both our teachers and our students.

Archetypes, Deities and Totems

Deities, archetypes and totems are aspects of our own nature, expressing themselves in a myriad of forms to teach us about ourselves.

According to Carl Jung, "The archetype is a tendency to form such representations of a motif—representations that can vary a great deal in detail without losing their basic pattern...they also manifest themselves in fantasies and often reveal their presence only by symbolic images. . .They are without known origin; and they reproduce themselves in any time or in any part of the world—even where transmission by direct descent or 'cross fertilization' through migration must be ruled out."[1]

This over-riding, broad manifestation of a principle is expressed in the primal images of archetypes. An example of a personal and strong image that is true for everybody is the Great Mother. When archetypal images are personified as active manifestations they are seen as the individualized presence of a deity. The Great Mother is an archetype, and yet her manifestations in personal images and personal or cultural deities number in the thousands. The Egyptian goddess Isis has been called the "Lady of 2,000 names." Whether She is presented in the form of the Chinese Quan Yin, or the Tibetin Green Tara, or the Christian Mother Mary, she represents total compassion.

Deities are the intermediaries between universal principles and ourselves. Love and compassion, for instance, are archetypal qualities. To divide them into individual aspects is to create deities. There are many different deities to represent all the aspects of the universal archetypes, and they have different qualities in the different cultures. The deities personify those aspects so that we can emulate them. They show us the highest development of these energies in terms we can understand. By following their examples we experience the emotion and path of wisdom they personify.

Totems depict the universal principles in a more worldly form, as expressions of nature with fewer cultural overtones. They tend to be tribal and present themselves as guides, friends or allies.We can make agreements with a totem ally and do things together. It assists us in our lives. If, for example, you are hunting, a totem can be a spirit ally who will help you in your pursuit. Each totem enjoys certain activities in accordance with its nature. It helps us to express ourselves in ways that are active, both mentally and physically.

Every animal manifestation in Egypt has a deity form as well. The god Thoth is a personification of the archetypes of wisdom and healing. He also has the aspects of the totem bird, the ibis, and through this form he shows us which actions we can take to become wise.

Archetypes are universal, deities are specific to cultures. When you cry out to the Universe for love, one aspect will present itself to you in accordance with your receptivity.

There are many keys that open our awareness to these entities on the inner planes. Most basic is that when the student is ready, the teacher will appear. My Egyptian Huna and Cauldron work has led me to the discovery of deities and totems as guides to personal awakening and knowledge. These spiritual entities are available to all who, with intention and sincerity, invoke their presence. Who are these entities? Where are they? How can we interact with them to further our own development?

These beings are composites of the whole creation, whose propensity to display certain aspects of nature defines their role. We are much the same. Within each of us is a host of characters, some more prominent than others. It is the balanced integration and dominion over the multitudes of characters within us that gives us mastery. Each of these characters has its own special knowledge, whether it be a Buddha, a Christ or a cobbler. As we become more aware we can consciously call forth these inner personalities, these aspects of our own natures when we need them to deal with a situation or to learn the lesson of any given moment. Then archetypal representations, those beings who usually remain in the background, will come to the fore.

The deities are image guides who help us to establish a norm that we can focus on when we interact with them. They project to us the images that have been left for us by our ancestors. In my view of reality, the Earth is our Mother, a living, breathing entity, and all living things that share this planet with us are our relatives. The images that have been passed down to us have been catalogued in the rich history of mythology and legend. In our technological age we can look back through history and trace the evolution of the archetypes from their most ancient anonimity, through diverse cultural changes and traditions and into a present rich with the multiplicity of cultural variety.

We choose images that are appropriate for our purposes at any given moment. If our concern is with knowledge, we attract images that will direct us to the sources of the knowledge we seek. By moving back to our primal source we envision each entity we encounter as a guide, a statement of proper action.

In my inner planes research I have been drawn primarily to the Egyptian images, because even though the names and prominence of the deities were constantly changing, there is a certain stability to the natural aspects, the animal forms on which the deities are based. The Egyptian gods and goddesses are depicted with a mixture of anthropomorphic and animal characteristics. Animal heads rest on human bodies or human heads on animal bodies. Sometimes a mixture of animal parts make up a composite entity, or an associated animal is used as the headress of a human form. The Sphinx is one such composite form. We respond to animal images because they symbolize complex human attributes, attributes held in esteem by human groups.

In Egyptian theology, there is a spirit manifest in all forms of life, which is its *neter,* or god-self. All animals can be depended upon to function in accordance with their own natures, and those deities that are associated with animal forms exhibit the animals' particular attributes. One of the predominant features of native tribal systems has been their association with totem animals. From the most ancient of times, clans and individuals have related to animal spirits as allies, sources of power.

We have whole groups of deities with whom to work. In the same way we view the many stars in the sky, we can choose to look to different entities to help us work through various situations in this lifetime in preparation for the future. There are entities to deal with every aspect of human nature, and you can choose the ones that you like, that have meaning for you.

As you learn to recognize the qualities of each deity you begin to understand why they are associated with particular totem animals. If you aspire to certain attributes you can choose to interact with the appropriate totem, the one that depicts those attributes.

In different parts of the world certain totems have predominance. There are places where different entities manifest as the strongest local totem because that is the nature of the people living there and their world. Every landscape offers many variations of life and each aspect of nature is represented by different combinations of awareness, expressing as a pantheon of gods. Some areas bear similarities to other areas, but each has its own unique manifestations. Because nature and cultures do bear similarities to each other, we find deities in different parts of the world who have similar attributes and expressions. Thus, we find Anubis, the jackal-headed god in Egypt, Coyote in America, the Wolf among the Eskimo and the Fox in Japan.

Following are some examples of deities and totems and their attributes. I also offer some "journeys," exercises that will give you direct experience of some of these entities. By connecting to and building rapport with these beings, you can find ways to enhance your present life and prepare for your future.

Thoth

Because I am a seeker of truth and wisdom, Thoth has become my primary guide. According to Egyptologist E.A. Wallis Budge, "The character of Thoth is a lofty and a beautiful conception, and is, perhaps, the highest idea of deity ever fashioned in the Egyptian mind."[2] He is the scribe of the Egyptian pantheon, god of wisdom, communications, healing magic, arts, sciences and more. Usually Thoth is represented by the ibis, the sacred bird of Africa, although he is known also as a baboon and sometimes as a cobra. The Greeks called Thoth Hermes, the Thrice Great Born; the Romans knew him as Mercury, messenger of the Gods.

You connect with Thoth through your desire to know. To be in a relationship with him is to have a great teacher, friend, healer and protector, for he personifies the mind of the creation. Thoth responds to those who, with sincerity and purpose, invoke his presence. He will respond in accordance with the receptivity of the individual; some people will see images, others will hear or feel his presence. You can call on the image of Thoth for inner light, inner enlightening. When you want all the attributes of understanding, healing, searching for the light, you can invoke the image of Thoth, and as you focus and become aware, the attributes of the Thoth entity can be felt. When hunting for schools of fish beneath the surface of the lake, the ibis will spread its wing to create a shadow through which he can see better into the depths of the water. So it is with the image of Thoth, who helps you see the way into the realm of inner senses when you are hunting for knowledge.

In my own quest I was initiated into awareness of Thoth, that is, I was introduced to him by another person. As our relationship developed, I was given a way to introduce others to this being, through an initiatory meditative journey called "The Cauldron of Thoth." This guided journey is a key into the experience and understanding of the deity and totem interaction which can be a great acceleration to the awakening process. For example, journeying with Ganesh, the Hindu Elephant God, can teach you to expedite the process of manifestation, bringing into physical form what you want in your future.

The Cauldron is a symbol for the vessel that we are, for each of us contains the creative forces of life within us. We are that sacred grail within whose primordial waters churns the whole of the collective consciousness, and we can nourish ourselves from its rich and vital contents. All knowledge is within ourselves. As you continue your search for the keys that unlock the knowledge within, you will find symbols that, as you focus your attention on them, resonate to clear your path and open the way. With Thoth as your guide, stir the contents of your own cauldron and safely explore the myriad of possibilities within.

Thoth has dominion over the other deity and totem forms, for he is the keeper of the records, the scribe. Communication is power, and he is lord of both language and writing. The ibis or crane can be imaged as the guide that takes you to the other attributes, such as the bear, the mother vulture, the eagle, hawk, elephant, or to the Akashic records.

The initiating journey into the teachings of the Cauldron has been recorded with an accompanying musical score by John Sergeant and is available on cassette tape.[3] In "The Cauldron of Thoth, a Journey of Empowerment," you are introduced to a way of altering your own consciousness to relate to specific entities and experiences. You meet Thoth and are directed to Mut, the Egyptian Mother Goddess, and to the Crone, the wise, old woman in each of us who is our initiator.

The following journey is the initiation into "The Cauldron of Thoth." You may wish to have someone read it aloud to you, leaving appropriate spaces for your individual experience. You can make your own tape recording of it in your own voice, or, for optimum results, you can purchase the tape that I've produced for that purpose. The first time you take the initiatory journey it is best to sit up or stand. Be sure to allow yourself time to experience fully between each instruction. Your environment is also very important, so choose a quiet, meditative place where you will not be interrupted.

The Cauldron of Thoth

Close your eyes, relax and breathe deeply. Inhale through the small of your back, filling your belly, and exhale through your tailbone into the Earth, deepening your connection to the Earth, grounding and centering yourself in preparation for your travels into realms beyond space, beyond time... Feel the cycles of your breath. Feel as your body opens to new levels of sensitivity...

Now place your hands before you with the palms facing up to receive the gift that is coming to you... It is a purple-black egg, flecked in gold and it descends from above to rest gently in the palms of your hands. Notice its size, its weight, its substance. This is an etheric egg, an egg of creation... When you are sure of its presence, draw the egg into your abdomen, as though your abdomen is a womb waiting to receive and nurture the egg that you have been given...

Focus your attention now upon your heart center. Look deep within your own heart to find the eternal flame that burns within you. As you focus on your inner heart flame, begin directing love to it to make it grow and *feel* as the radiant warmth and light from your heart flame spreads to illuminate your entire being...

Bring your attention to the top of your head and you will feel as a crown comes down to rest gently upon your crown chakra, around the top of your head. Notice what it looks like and how it feels. Notice what it is made of. This crown marks the empowerment you are receiving at this time and provides the portal through which you will travel out of and back into your body...

Look once more to see and feel the egg that has been gestating within the womb of your being. You will feel its outer shell being absorbed into your abdominal walls, revealing the cauldron within. This cauldron is the source of all life, all wisdom. Feel it expand inside you to fill your abdomen. The primordial oceans of creation, the waters of life reside within your cauldron. It contains all of the cycles of regeneration, all emotions and the whole of the collective consciousness...

Begin to stir the waters of life in your cauldron. As you stir these waters, the waters begin to rise. As the waters within the cauldron rise, they come into contact with the flame in the heart, and there is a great hissing, bubbling and crackling, as the water hits the flame and converts to steam. And then the steam begins to rise, and as the steam rises, it opens the passageway in your throat and begins to fill your head. Let your conscious rise with the steam. Let it merge with the steam in your head. Focus all of your attention, all of your consciousness within this steam, and as the pressure builds, the steam will lift you and you will rise with the steam right up out of your body through your crown, in your light body and hover there, above your physical form...

Look now to your left and you will see your guide, the one who will always be here to help you when you journey in this way. Most often it is Thoth, the ibis-headed scribe of the Egyptian pantheon. Greet this guide with respect, and request passage into the domain of the Crone...

Thoth points his staff and when you look toward where he is pointing, there is a resplendent vulture. This is Mut, the ancient Mother Goddess, mother of all. She is the primordial mother of the pantheon of Egypt, noble in her character and stature. Mut lifts you gently into flight and carries you across the wonderous vistas of our Mother Earth. Mut flies you over many different landscapes of incredible beauty, soaring on the currents of the wind as she carries you over mountains and valleys, canyons of indescribable beauty, forests and deserts, and the great waters, the rivers, lakes and oceans. She is taking you to her secret place. The entrance to her sacred temple is hidden, covered by lush green foliage, marked by clear water near its narrow opening. She flies down with you and you enter into the Earth, through the dark, narrow opening passageway, downward, as she descends, until she sets you down gently at the bottom of a large cavern, the womb of Mother Earth. As she points upward to the ceiling, this cavern lights up with a soft warm glow so that you can see around you. Notice the details of this womb, what it looks like and feels like, its colors and textures. Open all of your senses. Listen to the sounds and you will hear the sound of running water coming from a niche where it flows sweetly and softly from the walls of the cave. You must cleanse and purify yourself in these waters in preparation for the next stage of your journey...

When you have purified yourself in the flowing waters of the womb, return to the cavern and you will see the Crone. She is old beyond time. The embodiment of divine wisdom, this wise, old woman is so very old that you know she has been priestess of Mut for thousands of years. And yet there is a familiarity about her. She is very pleased to see you and conveys to you a feeling of specialness for having made this journey. She sets about placing a circle of crystals in the center of the cavern. As she places each crystal, it becomes a light until there is a sacred circle of glowing crystal lights...

She beckons you into the center, and the ground churns beneath your feet, within this sacred circle. And yet, you maintain your balance upon the undulating Earth. As you stand before the Crone, she reaches into a fold in her garment and brings forth a magical stone, which she places in your third eye. This stone is the universal medicine, the healing stone. It contains all knowledge of the Earth, and its nature is revealed through experience. Feel this stone enter and begin to awaken ancient memories and long forgotten knowledge...

And now the Crone presents you with an herb, a plant that is a power plant for you. It may be the entire plant, or a portion of it, a blossom, a leaf, a root. As you receive this plant, its essence feeds you with awareness of its nature. Its spirit permeates your being and you feel it in all the cells of your body. You feel and you understand its power. You smell its fragrance and your mouth is filled with its taste, the taste of your new ally. You will know how to use this herb for healing yourself or others, and you know that the Crone is the keeper of the storehouse of herbal knowledge. You may always come to her to learn more about plants and their uses...

You are very grateful for the gifts the Crone has given to you and so you may wish to give her a gift as an offering. If so, choose an aspect of yourself, of your physical being or your character to give to her in support of the work that she is doing...

The Crone is pleased. She has yet another special gift for you at this time; an instruction or initiation that is just for you according to your own readiness or personal commitment. Receive what she gives to you now...(long pause)

When this time with the Crone is complete you have only to look deep within her eyes and she will turn back into Mut, the vulture goddess who will lift you gently, flying upward, up through the dark, narrow passageway and out once more over the wonderous vistas of our Mother Earth. As you're flying with Mut, look down at the terrain over which you fly and notice the difference in your perception... You are flying back to the gateway where Thoth has been guarding your body while you have been journeying in this way. You may wish to give him a gift to show your respect and gratitude...

Thoth will show you the way back into your body through your crown. Feel yourself connect with your physical body... Take a moment to ground and center yourself, feeling yourself solidly within your body. And when you're ready, open your eyes.

It is a good idea to write down your journeys immediately after you've returned if possible. Sometimes you receive messages that will become clearer during a future meditation.

Use the first part of the above journey, the alchemy, to change your dimension and access Thoth each time you wish to use this technique. You already have the Cauldron, so you no longer need to receive the egg or the crown. It is always important to start with the grounding breath and to spend a moment sending love to your inner heart flame.

Journeys with Totem Animals

Deities and totems of all cultures and traditions are available through the Cauldron and Thoth. Using this form, you can look through the eyes of the totems and deities to see the world as they see it. Using their perspective can enable you to gain insight into your current life, or even to project into the future to find answers.

The Nile is like the spinal column of the Earth, the main channel through which the lifeforce of the Earth passes. Just as in the human body, there are chakra centers along the Earth's spine. These centers are associated with particular deities, and so have their representative totem animals. By seeing with the eyes of the various deities in the Egyptian pantheon you can experience the energies of the chakras of the Nile.

Many cultures have used masks to depict their divinities; the Greeks donned the masks that represented their gods, the Native American shamans wore totem headresses or animal masks or robes. When you cloak yourself in the image of a totem it is like putting on its mask, its energy. This enables you to travel with its spirit. The feathers of the eagle, the robe of the buffalo, or the invocation of Anubis will provide you with the unique vantage point of that entity. You can use a physical mask or visualize the image as a way of achieving the feelings that enhance the process. The mask actually is the symbol or metaphor for the viewpoint of a particular entity.

The idea is to come from your own root, your own origin, and then interact with or merge with the entity of your choice, but FROM YOURSELF. We are here to experience, to be whatever we can, and to undertake tasks and challenges that will help us learn and grow in wisdom. We can choose the path of return or the path of the spirit where we can open to the myriad masks of ourselves. In this unfolding there are master craftspersons who have fashioned masks that they will allow us to wear.

Anubis

You may choose to put on the mask or headress of Anubis, the jackel, and through his eyes see his enlightened view, characteristic and unique. In Egyptian theology, Anubis is the one who reads the scales at death. (When a person dies s/he is brought before the scales of Thoth and his/her heart is weighed against the feather of Maat, the goddess who represents truth and justice.) When you visit Anubis, you experience his perspective of reality. He manifests a keenness of hearing, extreme clarity, a sharp sense of smell, and the ability to differentiate the various sources of light and darkness. His sight sees all colors, dark or light, and he moves almost with the swiftness of thought. Without taking time to ponder, his awareness to act is instinctual. Anubis is a teacher, and through his eyes, you receive education, learning and protection. He guides people, bringing them through the darkness and back into the light. Many people fear the darkness, but knowing that there is a guide to aid you can bring a great deal of comfort. By visiting Anubis you acquire knowledge, and you may keep or discard what you have learned when you take off his mask, his world view.

To find Anubis through the Cauldron process, you will be sent by Thoth into the darkness of the night to seek out the glowing eyes of the jackel who hides in the shadows. It is always best to have an intention or specific question in mind when seeking the guidance of Anubis.

Ganesh, the Elephant Goddess

When someone wants to change his/her life there is a solution, there is a way. Sometimes the desire and the means are easy to match. Other times it is more difficult. Things happen in certain unpredictable progressions. We are involved in this interaction with life and as we become more aware we realize there are different progressions we can choose. We are not the masters of creation itself, we are part of creation, which is why we encounter accidents and unplanned events.

We must deal with the problems that face us now so that there will be a future for posterity. Each generation has special, overwhelming challenges with which it must deal. What we desire for our future comes from our memory. Although we wish for the best we cannot expect that to be the future. The future is the past if you view time as a circle rather than a straight line. The way to shape your future is to try to move in a spiral, which is how you move through time. As we ponder the unknown, we can focus our intentions to envision a desirable future. Though we move forward with the intent of world peace we may never realize it in its completion, but we will move forward in that direction through our intent. We can use intelligence and consciousness for achieving goals while we have the opportunity.

The Hindus have a deity named Ganesh who is the child of Shiva. This being has a royal intelligence and when you come into his/her presence s/he will help you shoulder your burdens. S/he is lord of solutions and brings great peace and tranquility. When you have a great task, call on Ganesh and s/he will help you find the path through your obstacles. S/he helps you resolve your troubles. If you're starting a task s/he can help you to get going, to take each step and to see ahead with your intellect. You can use the following journey with Ganesh to help you to manifest your goals, and to see into the future.

In all instances, it is best to have a specific purpose that is compatible with the nature of the being you are visiting. For this journey you can choose to work with a goal or an obstacle. You can focus on immediate or long-range plans. Ganesh also can help you manifest the things you need in your life. Through the realizations of your wants, needs and desires you will be able to see into the future, unencumbered by hopes, fears and concerns of the present. Learn from Ganesh how to get what you want and then look to the future to see what lies beyond your expectations. If you choose, you will see into the future, then from that place you can look back on the questions of today with a broader perspective and the wisdom of hindsight.

Once again, you may wish to make a tape of this journey, leaving pauses or using your pause button to give yourself time between instructions. Or have someone read it to you in the appropriate time and setting.

To visit Ganesh, use your cauldron to get to Thoth. Start by closing your eyes. Relax...ground and center with your breath, inhaling through the small of your back and exhaling into the Earth through your tailbone... Devote attention to your inner heart flame... Direct love to it to make it grow, and feel the radiance from your heart flame expand to fill your entire being... Stir the waters of life within your cauldron and as the waters rise, hear and feel as the waters come in contact with the heart flame and turn to steam... Let your conscious-ness rise with the steam as it moves upward, opens the passage at your throat and fills your head... Then focus all your attention into the steam and lift right up through your crown in your light body, and look to your left where Thoth awaits... Greet Thoth and he will point the way to Ganesh...

You first see the eyes, big, intelligent, willing to share your burden. As you look into the eyes of your elephant, tell him/her your problem, or what you would like to accomplish. Then his/her form comes into view and you are aware of the night sky, with a moon and blanket of stars—then the Earth. You hear in the distance the music of hand cymbals and dancing feet.

You have entered the realm of Ganesh, the elephant God/dess. Here all your burdens become light. The elephant drops to one knee and you climb onto his/her back. Sit in comfort, arms out to your sides, thumbs covering index fingernails, chest forward, head back.

The elephant begins to take you on a walk through nature. Imagine the elephant's head coming from your chest as you rock from side to side, swaying in a figure eight, as you ride the elephant through the thickest of bushes, forests or jungle. No obstacles halt the elephant. The elephant is showing you how to take each step as you continue to sway...

You are following your heart's desire and allowing your intellect to help you find the correct, balanced path. As you sway with the motion of the elephant, chest forward, you feel the elephant's heart as your own, and your heart naturally begins to open...

The terrain grows steeper, the path more rigorous and narrow. Still the elephant continues, step after step. As you continue you receive an intellectual awareness of what to do or an intellectual understanding of your life problem or situation. It's connected to following your heart, being centered and at peace within your heart.

Dawn is breaking, and at first light you begin to get a sense of the immediate steps you must take to clear the problem or achieve your goals. As you sway with the elephant, s/he clears your path. By the time you've reached the top of the mountain, your heart is fully open. You've merged with, become one with the elephant.

Ganesh stops on the peak of the mountain and you look through his/her eyes to see where s/he is looking across the new horizon. You have stopped swaying. Feel your love for Mother Earth as you look toward the sunrise. The first ray of sunlight appears and strikes your third eye. Allow yourself to experience the full impact and intensity of the sunlight as it penetrates your third eye for the time it takes for the sun to rise...

Extend your chest, open your arms wide with your palms up as you take the breathing stance. As the horizon opens before you, take five deep breaths, throwing your head and trunk back with each inhale through your nose, and blowing out the breath from your mouth as you bring your head forward...

At the end of the fifth breath, either drop forward, third eye to the floor or lie on your back. Keep still. With your final exhale let yourself float and allow whatever will to happen. As you take off, relax and enjoy whatever comes up. Allow your vision to carry you into the future. The elephant has cleared your path and shown you the way. You now have a chance to explore. Fly into the horizon. Look beyond your expectations. Stay as long as you are comfortable (three minutes is enough to experience quite a bit here)...

To come back, think of the elephant's eyes. S/he will be there sitting on the mountain top, and you are sitting in his/her lap, between his/her legs, which become pillars of your own personal temple...

As you return down the path in the light of the new day, there are no obstacles. Thoth meets you on the way and shows you back to your body through your crown. Remember to use the grounding breath and be sure you are fully centered and connected with your physical form before opening your eyes.

Eawokka, the Bear

Some entities can teach you specifically about healing. Thoth is a good one for that, because understanding and knowledge naturally result in healing. The bear is another one. The bear is a helpful ally because she is familiar with the ways of nature, the herbs and the crystals that are found deep within the caves where she makes her home. I have a wonderful relationship with a particular cinnamon grizzly she-bear from the north, where it's very cold and where there exist crystals never before experienced by humans. Eawokka, the bear, assists me in my teaching and healing work. Her deft claws have performed meticulous psychic surgical procedures when, on occasion, we work as a healing team. This bear also works very well with children.

Please be particularly courteous during the winter, when bears hibernate, for you can imagine that a bear might be grumpy when awakened! She may even choose to replace herself during that period with some other entity that will be appropriate to your goal; or you might meet her friend, Eeta, the hedgehog, who sometimes speaks for her in the winter. If appropriate, you will have access to the crystals she keeps in her home. Be very sensitive during hibernation time to stay only as long as absolutely necessary, although at other times of the year her teachings can be quite lengthy.

This journey will give you an introduction to working with crystals and help you to increase your awareness of our planet as a living entity. Even those of you who understand the theory of the Earth as a living being usually have not felt it in your bodies, hearts and bones. Helping you to experience this is Eowokka's primary function. Once you have felt the pulse beat of the Mother through every cell of your being, you will never again be without awareness of the rhythm that connects you to all things. Your emotional body can be thoroughly healed by the recognition of your resonance, your link with that pulse beat. Allow it to become a part of your being. Never again must you feel alone or apart from the Earth. You begin to grasp the meaning of time, the inhaling and exhaling of breath like the waves of the ocean, the tides of the Earth. It's like putting your head next to the heartbeat of the one you love. Having experienced that resolution, you will always feel connected to the life force. Put your bare feet in the dirt often to feel and remember the pulse beat of Mother Earth.

To take a journey through the Cauldron with the bear, either make a tape of the journey or have someone read it to you, leaving appropriate pauses. Take the time to relax, ground and center, using the grounding breath from the first exercise... Focus attention to your inner heart flame with love, feeling the flame expand and radiate through your being... Stir the waters in your cauldron... Notice the waters rise to meet the flame in the heart and turn to steam... Move with the steam through the opening in the throat and into your head... Focus your consciousness into the steam and rise up through your crown in your light body. Thoth is on your left. . .Greet him and ask to visit Eawokka, the Bear of the Night Sky...

Thoth points the way to the home of the bear, in the dark, cold realms to the north. You find yourself in the distant land of ice and crystals, a mountainous terrain. You make your way to the mouth of her cave, and there you listen... You can hear her inside. She is moving in a rocking motion back and forth, side to side, drumming, boom...boom...boom..., to put you in touch with the heartbeat of the planet Earth. Listen and allow yourself to come into resonance with the pulse of the Mother...(allow a long pause here)

When you feel that pulse throughout your whole being, call out the name of Eawokka three times and she will amble out of her cave to greet you... Around her neck, hung from a red strap, is a solid gold medallion cast with the image of a turtle. Greet Eawokka. She might let you climb on her back and hold the strap of the medallion like reins as she takes you on a journey, or she may invite you into her home and share with you her crystals and the knowledge of how to use them. She will take you through an experience that will answer whatever questions you have brought with you. (Allow yourself as much time as you need to complete the journey she gives you.)

You may wish to give her a gift to help sustain her in her work.

When your time is complete, follow the path back to where Thoth awaits, to guide you back into your body. Be sure to take time to ground and center yourself in your body before opening your eyes.

The Snow Leopard

There will come a time when you must deal with the darker aspects of your life, when you are forced to face your innermost fears. Only when you have finally stopped running, have looked at your fear and found that place in you that knows you have no alternative but to stand fully firm and face it directly does fear become your ally. The Snow Leopard can take you places and teach you things that you can only learn through fear. This is not a lengthy journey, only an introduction, yet you should allow yourself sufficient time to *feel* the nuances of the experience. You can probably do this as an exercise without the assistance of tape or reader. Try reading it over and then taking the journey on your own.

Following is an introduction to the Snow Leopard. You must first move through the process of the alchemy, grounding and centering..., feeding your inner heart flame with love..., stirring the waters of your cauldron until they lift to meet the flame within your heart... Follow the steam that is created by the union of the fire and water, aware of the opening of your throat as the steam passes up into your head. Focus your attention within that steam and move straight up through your crown into your light body... Thoth will be on your left. Tell him you wish to learn from the Snow Leopard... He will direct you to a doorway that is a rite of passage.

When you enter through the door into the darkness you will hear a sound that is beyond a roar. It is higher in pitch. You are struck by a sense of fear. Notice where those feelings are in your body. Notice your pulse rate, your breathing. The cry of the Snow Leopard continues. What is your first thought? To hide? To defend yourself? What are your first feelings, your instinctual reactions? Recognize your own instinct. Experience it and act out your instinct. Hide, or make a weapon, or run, or stand frozen, defacating in your own terror... When you have been forced to face yourself as you are, you will see two glowing, golden eyes glaring at you through the darkness. When you see the eyes shining out of the darkness, you will have reached the end of your first taste of the Snow Leopard. When you have reached the end you will sense a light behind you where before there was only darkness. This is the passageway out of the realm of the Snow Leopard. As you turn and walk toward the light, you know you will do so in safety... Thoth will be waiting to assist you back into your body, where you take a few grounding breaths and center yourself in your physical form.

When you again journey with the Snow Leopard, you will step beyond the point you have already experienced. This is a preview, a forewarning of what is to come. The next lesson is whether your fear inhibits you from experiencing the rest of the journey, or, if you are truly courageous and desire the knowledge that comes with the experience of fear.

Exploring the Spirit World

Throughout history, in cultures as diverse as the Egyptians, the Native Americans of North and South America, the

Eskimos and the Mongolians, there have been shamanistic traditions. One of the predominent features of these tribal systems has been their association with totem animals. Back to the most ancient of times, clans and individuals related to animal spirits as allies, as sources of power. One of the things that distinguished the *shaman* is his/her ability to use the inner senses to traverse the dimensions of consciousness in order to explore realms beyond ordinary reality. It is the function of the shaman to find the means for change in our physical world by working directly with the intelligent and elemental aspects of the spirit world. A common thread in shamanism is the archetypal quality of the experiences, and the universal symbolism that this deep inner work evokes.

Movement, sound, most often percussion or song, and states of ecstacy are the domain of the shaman. S/he is healer and mystic, and comes into power through bloodlines, dreams, illness or ordeal. The shaman is one who has faced death, usually through encounters within the spiritual realms where s/he is dismembered or devoured, and mastered it. The subsequent rebirth brings with it insight and power. The vision and awareness acquired in this way are fundamental to the work of mediating between our ordinary reality and the spirit world.

Modern day explorers of the inner planes encounter similar visionary experiences when they probe the depths of the mysteries. Each undergoes a rite of passage, a journey from the outer senses through to the light of inner vision. This requires actively invoking inner awareness, memory and creativity, inner senses.

Intuition is both an inner and outer sense. We allow ourselves to change and grow through our intuition. We gain vision by accepting our inner senses. On the physical plane we "follow our noses," on the inner plane we use our intuition.

When we become aware of other entities on the astral, or find ourselves in strange situations in the physical, or if we simply want to find out more about something, we can call up any image, any entity, perhaps one of those we met in the Cauldron "journeys." We can draw up the image from memory and go directly to it.

When we relate to the deity forms we relate to our innerselves and we start from our original Self, which is the same for all of us. We return to our original state, beyond form and time, where we are once again one with the Light. All things are eminations of that Light. If we want to experience other entities on other planes of existence we go back to the common denominator of light, and then follow our intuition and creativity to make them into a mental form. It's as if we are blindfolded, reaching into the dark to feel the face of another, and through that feeling come to an interpretation. This is the difference between seeing something with our physical eyes and psychically or astrally seeing by using our intuition and creativity.

One way to perceive of the deities is as your highest self. We tend to anthropomorphize deities, and we expect them to be like humans. These deities, many faces of your higher self, are here to guide you in your mission on Earth, through the tasks and challenges of this lifetime and into the next. Most of us come into physical life with a purpose that we chose for ourselves, although some do not have the opportunity to choose. Before we were born we may have chosen a hope or goal; we may or may not attain that hope or goal in this lifetime. How we pursue that goal and the motivation that drives us, however, affects not only our present lifetimes, but our future ones as well.

Time Traveling in the Spirit World

Try drawing a picture of something based on your feeling of it. Then compare your picture with what your physical eyes see.

You can use this technique as a way of corroborating astral travel. You can astral travel to some place far away—in space or time—and draw a picture based on your feelings and emotions. If that place exists now you can physically go there or find a photograph and see if your vision matches. If that place exists some time in the future, you can save your picture until the appropriate time then compare your vision with what comes into physical being later.

There are specific exercises we can do that will show us the way to the inner self, back to the simple, unmanifest presence of nonform. To get into the next life, we must go back to our Source and manifest from that Source as we choose, or in accordance with what we have created for ourselves. In this state we can accept all that we are and all that we know, and by accepting all that we don't know we can invoke new knowledge, create new experiences. It is by returning to our most fundamental common denominator—light itself—that we can reach out to interact with all that is within. That state is often called our "light body," and is the state of mobility we reach when we do the alchemy of the Cauldron. Try this next journey to perceive yourself outside of the ordinary constraints of space and time.

Thoth's Magic Diamond

Close your eyes, relax and breathe deeply, using your grounding breath to prepare for this journey. Proceed with the alchemy (see previous instructions)...

When you get up to Thoth, he is pleased that you have returned, and he has a special gift for you. Thoth hands you a magic diamond, a sparkling stone with many facets. Each facet of this diamond is a window; each provides a different view. As you study your new tool, focus through it upon your physical body, as though it were a microscope, revealing a different depth of field with each turn... You begin to perceive your body as a landscape. As seen from above, its surface textures create geometric forms... As you look deeper, the images change, you pass through starburst patterns of energy, and as you continue to turn your diamond, it reveals a yet deeper field of focus, until you find yourself gazing into the night sky, spangled with stars...

As above, so below; you recognize yourself, and the Universe within you. Each star, each cell of your body is a sun with revolving planets, peopled with abundant life forms. You are God or Goddess of your own Universe. It's your responsibility to enlighten all life within you, and so you begin to radiate unconditional love energy through your magic diamond, into the field beneath you, generating all the colors of the rainbow into every cell in this way, charging all life within with the radiant light of love...

This energy, this love that you have sent forth, is reflected back to you, magnified by the magic diamond and you experience waves of bliss and shivers of joy as that which you have sent out returns to you. Feel as it tingles and awakens every cell of your being...(long pause)

Begin to reverse your diamond, observing your body becoming solid once more, window by window as you return through the different levels of perception.

Now take a moment to explore another window, another facet of your magic diamond. You will discover that with focused intention, you can find a window that will take you into your future, or your past, to explore other lifetimes...(long pause)

Know that you can come back often to discover the many possibilities and uses for this wonderful tool. Take a moment to converse with Thoth and receive further guidance as to your use of the gifts of the Cauldron...

You may wish to ask Thoth if there is something that you can do for him...

Thoth will guide you back into your body through your crown. Be sure to take a few grounding breaths to assure that you are fully connected with and centered in your physical form before opening your eyes.

When questing in this way, it is best to have a purpose, and so you could ask, "Of what benefit will this work be to my future, and my future lives? What's left to be done? Need I come back at all?"

If you could honestly evaluate where you are and determine what it would be like to have all your desires met, all goals and needs accomplished, what would it feel like? Can you see yourself having completed everything in this lifetime?

Your divinity is complete. Total knowledge and awareness is and has always been complete. The shell of ignorance may go. *Command it away!* Look to those around you and see the light of allness within. Acknowledge, feed, and grow. *Notice:* only the shells age. *Notice:* the unity of life is all inclusive.

The goal of this work is to develop yourself, unique and aware, to move from the apprentice to the journeyperson to the true accomplishment of being yourself. Life is a work of art, which we can create consciously. If we remain unconscious life still reveals itself as a work of art. The difference between our conscious and unconscious living is like the difference between sleepwalking and creating a piece of beauty as an artist. This is the craft, or artistry which we learn from the master artisans. From these deities and totem allys we learn that we can create in this life. Look upon these entities, gods and goddesses as craftpersons who are willing to share their unique outlooks so that we may join them in conscious creative livingas independent and aware individuals, willingly committed to the ongoing dance of life on Earth.

Notes

1. Carl G. Jung, *Man and His Symbols* (New York: Doubleday Publishing Co., 1969), p.58.
2. E.A. Wallis Budge, *The Gods of the Egyptians,* Vol. 1 (New York: Dover Publications, Inc., 1969), p.415
3. Nicki Scully, with John Sergeant, *The Cauldron of Thoth* (ASCAP, Plumrose Music Unltd.)

Our Future Lives in the Age of Aquarius

6

by Mary Devlin

From the beginning of time human beings have been fascinated
with the sky and the celestial bodies that inhabited it. The
life-giving Sun, the silvery Moon who changed her shape as
she changed her position in the sky, the diamond-like stars in
the night sky must have inspired awe in the hearts and minds
of our ancestors, leading them to wonder: What is my place in
the Universe? How does this all relate to me? As early peoples
began to observe correlations between activity in the heavens
and events on Earth, the twin science/arts of astrology and
astronomy were born. (It wasn't until about the seventeenth
century that the two were separated.) For thousands of years
we have continued to investigate, observe, study and expand
our knowledge of astrology and the Universe, and to use this
knowledge to enrich our lives.

Most people are familiar with the twelve signs of the zodiac:
Aries, Taurus, Gemini, Cancer, Leo, Virgo, Libra, Scorpio,
Sagittarius, Capricorn, Aquarius, and Pisces.

At the time of the earliest known written records the signs of
the zodiac corresponded roughly to twelve constellations in
the sky, known as the *zodiac noeta* or "knowable zodiac."

Because the Earth is not steady on its axis as it travels around the Sun, but rather wobbles a bit, the tropical zodiac—or the zodiac as measured by the seasons—no longer corresponds to the zodiac noeta. The two zodiacs have become virtually separate.

In the mid-twentieth century, Swiss psychologist/astrologer Carl Jung drew public attention to the phenomenon now called the Great Ages. Combining Hindu philosophy and his knowledge of astronomy and history, Jung observed that the position of the Sun at the vernal equinox (Aries) appeared to move backwards through each sign in the zodia noeta. When the vernal equinox coincided with a particular sign of the zodia noeta (as it does for a period of roughly two thousand years), the entire aura of that two-thousand-year period was colored by the characteristics associated with that sign.[1]

For example, the Age of Cancer (approximately 8000-6000 B.C.) was marked by widespread reverence for the Great Mother expressed by the worship of stones, trees and the Moon. The Age of Gemini brought the advent of writing and the worship of twin deities such as Castor and Pollux, or Apollo and Diana, and of two-faced gods like Janu or Janus. The Age of Taurus prompted the rise of practical art, such as interior decorating and architecture. The Age of Taurus was also marked by the worship of the bull—particularly in Crete and in ancient Egypt. According to some scholars the Biblical story in Exodus of the Israelites' worship of the Golden Calf was a throwback to Egyptian bull cults.[2] The Age of Aries was an era of conquest, exploration, and war, evidenced by the battles between Greece and Persia, between Rome and Carthage, and by the invasions of the Asian barbarians into Europe. The use of iron became widespread, particularly for weapons. At this time, the warrior-god-heroes, such as Krishna, Joshua, Achilles and Ulysses, became important. The beginnings of the Piscean Age marked the appearance of godlike figures who were hailed as savior-martyrs, the greatest of whom was Jesus of Nazareth. The aura of the Age of Pisces took on the characteristics associated with Jesus himself— faith, love, compassion, mysticism, and self-sacrifice.

Now we are on the verge of another Great Age: the Age of Aquarius. The position of the Sun at the vernal equinox has left the sign Pisces in the zodia noeta and is heading towards Aquarius. The symbol for Aquarius is human rather than animal: the Water-Carrier pouring the water of knowledge over the entire world. In this age, the sacred bull, the warrior god, the savior-martyr-heroes all will be gone. The God of the Aquarian Age is all of these and yet none of them. The Aquarian deity is the divinity within each human being, and the Age of Aquarius will emphasize respect for the lives and beliefs of others, by a new sense of fraternity. There will also be widespread expansion into the field of science (Aquarius is associated with progressive thought), but not at the expense of spiritual beliefs. Rather, the science of the Aquarian Age will serve to confirm spiritual beliefs, even as the new discoveries in quantum mechanics support the Hindu belief that all matter and energy are no more than pure consciousness.

Astrologers disagree about exactly when the Aquarian Age begins. Some believe that it began at the turn of this century; others say it started on February 4, 1962, when all the inner planets were in Aquarius, Uranus was in Leo, and the only two planets not involved in the configuration were Neptune and Pluto. Jose Arguelles, of "harmonic convergence" fame, says that according to the Mayan calendar, the world entered a new age on August 17, 1987; some believe this date marked the beginning of the Age of Aquarius. Vera Reid, author of *Towards Aquarius,* cites A.D. 2160, and Robert Hand, using exact astronomical measurements to chart the movements of the vernal equinox through the constellation Pisces, states that the Piscean Age will not end until 2813.[3]

This last date is rather sobering, but not all astrologers are convinced that the latter date is correct. My colleagues and I incline more towards a date sometime between now and Vera Reid's date. The constellations, though important as guide-posts, are strictly arbitrary, unequal in size and loosely constructed. Most of the stars in these constellations are not connected to each other in any way, meaning that they are not part of particular star clusters or binary systems. The outlines of these star patterns have been disputed over the years, and star charts show that the heavenly bodies involved in each have varied with the individuals who mapped the sky. Recent advances in physics, astronomy, and medicine, which appear to confirm ancient metaphysical beliefs, and the definite (though admittedly slow) changes in consciousness of the world population signify that we are indeed in a time of transition, even though it is difficult to pinpoint the exact moment we move from one age to the next.

Life in the Aquarian Age

This book is concerned with our future lives, and whatever the exact date on which we move from Pisces to Aquarius, our immediate future lives will take place in the Aquarian Age. So what exactly will the Aquarian Age involve? Many fine books have been written on the subject, generally taking the astrological attributes of the sign Aquarius and attaching them to the entire Age. The answer to that question, however, is much more complex than it appears on the surface; many factors have to be considered.

The best way to judge the coming Aquarian Age would be to consider the previous Aquarian Age and see what was happening then. But each Great Age lasts for approximately two thousand years, and there are twelve signs of the zodiac. Therefore, the previous Aquarian Age occurred between 25,000 and 22,000 B.C during the Upper Paleolithic period; the people of that era were pre-literate, and archaeological evidence is scant. Although present scientific dating methods are not exact, and we cannot say with absolute certainty, it may have been during this period when *homo sapiens* began to produce the breath-taking examples of cave art—at least, the earliest that we have are dated from that period. Tool-making seems to have reached a pinnacle during this epoch. It also appears to have been during this era that women first became aware of the synchronization of their bodies with the phases of the Moon, perhaps leading to the first systematic astrology. It is interesting to speculate that during the previous Aquarian Age, human beings first began not only to accumulate, but to apply knowledge and to use it to enrich and improve their lives. From evidence that many anthropologists believe signifies religious rites (some believe that the cave paintings depicting hunt scenes were magical in nature), it is also possible to deduce that during the previous Aquarian Age, the human race first became aware of its relationship with the cosmos.

If we are to judge the new Aquarian Age accurately, we must backtrack a little. With the dawn of the Age of Reason in the late seventeenth and early eighteenth centuries, it became fashionable to pooh-pooh any ideas of a spiritual Universe, and to treat science and metaphysics as separate and probably contradictory philosophies. The new discoveries of Newton and Galileo and later the theories of Darwin implied that the Earth was just a lump of rock, spinning aimlessly in space around the Sun, which would eventually burn itself out. Life itself was a cosmic accident, and we were not created separately, to be lords over nature, but actually descended from other animals. The fear and distrust predominant in the Piscean Age caused people to turn their fear and distrust even on God—and to doubt the very existence of a Divine force in the Universe.

I believe that the first glimmerings of the Aquarian Age were felt when this point of view was in vogue. Aquarius is associated with pure science, and the first appearances of the dominance of rational thought were indicative of an approaching change of consciousness. But this was only the beginning of Aquarian thought. For even though the Aquarian does cherish science and reason for their own sake, the Aquarian does not make a religion out of science, as the empirical scientists did for so long. The Aquarian believes in expansion of thought and of ideas, and does not put limitations on the expansion of thought. The Aquarian seeks to increase human knowledge at all costs, even if it means letting go of long-cherished concepts.

Aquarian science, despite its rationality, has more than a few elements of mysticism. Physicists, in searching for the primal subatomic particle—the so-called "seat of all existence"—have failed, apparently because there doesn't seem to be any primal particle. No matter how many times the physicists try to divide and subdivide the atom, they keep discovering more subatomic particles and rays, each with a different function all its own. And since all matter and energy are composed of the same subatomic particles, it seems that science has finally confirmed what the Masters have been teaching for thousands of years: All is one. We are all of the same essence.

One of the earliest champions of the new physics was Fritjof Capra, author of *The Tao of Physics*. Capra, a philosopher as well as a scientist, reported that his first transcendental experience occurred one day when he was sitting on the beach, watching as the surf rolled in and the foam covered the sand. He noticed that the rhythm of his breathing was synchronized with the motion of the sea, and then suddenly he realized that the entire rhythm around him was no less than the pulsating of the cosmos.

I "saw" cascades of energy coming down from outer space in which particles were created and destroyed in rhythmic pulses. I "saw" the atoms of the elements and those of my body participating in this cosmic dance of energy; I felt its rhythm and I "heard" its sound, and at that moment, I knew this was the Dance of Shiva.[4]

Scientists who have been a part of the conservative scientific establishment are becoming aware of the true relationship between humanity and the cosmos and, as a result, are participating in activities that are more "new age" in nature. Among these are astronauts Buzz Aldrin and Edgar Mitchell, who were two of the first to experience walking on the Moon. According to these astronauts, viewing the Earth from space was akin to Capra's revelation:

[Seeing the Earth from space] is a rather profound shift in consciousness . . . that makes us describe Earth without boundaries. . . . My own personal experience . . . was seeing that the Universe is indeed intelligent . . . of identification with the Universe itself, the joyous feeling of being a part of all that is.[5]

Medicine, too, is changing. Many younger doctors are less cold and distant than their older predecessors, and more inclined to see their patients as entire beings rather than as case histories. These doctors are more likely to consider the social, emotional, and psychological factors in illness and treat these factors along with the physical symptoms. The new doctors are also willing to explore the possibilities of alternative methods of healing, such as homeopathy, herbs, and acupuncture, and to view surgery and drugs as last-resort measures.

In the Age of Aquarius politics and the social structure will change as well.

The main concern of our long-ago ancestors was their own survival. At some point, human beings discovered that "there is safety in numbers" and began to band together, first in tribes, then in nations. Later, this tendency to band together grew into nationalism and pride in one's homeland: "my country, right or wrong." Foreigners, especially those who spoke another language or whose skin was a different color were not to be trusted.

This distrust is rapidly changing. The boundaries between nations and the differences in cultures are becoming less pronounced. Some people believe that governments in the Aquarian Age will be less competitive and more cooperative, eventually leading to a United Earth. The optimum level of political consciousness for the Aquarian Age is one world, one people.

Humanitarian movements, such as labor unions and charitable organizations, are also associated with Aquarius, and we will probably see more of those coming into being in the future. These movements are more effective when each individual involved has reached a state of relative inner peace and happiness.

The Civil Rights Movement and the Women's Movement of the 1960s are already well documented. More recently people have begun to support the rights of children. Organizations such as Greenpeace and the American Anti-Vivisection Society are speaking out for animals, who cannot speak for themselves, and people like Cleve Backster are expressing belief in the rights of plants. The recent attempts of millions to help those starving in Ethiopia has been followed by equally strong drives to help the homeless, the missing, and the victims of diseases such as AIDS. Millions have come together to help those less fortunate than themselves, and as the years go by, this humanitarian energy will increase. In the words of John Donne, we now know: "No man is an island, entire of itself." This is Aquarius, not next year, not in 2160, not in 2813, but *now*.

Even those involved in spiritual pursuits are experiencing a change in consciousness. We should pause here for a moment to draw a distinction between *spiritual* knowledge and *religious* knowledge. Religious knowledge is that in which an individual bases personal beliefs upon the experience of someone else. Spiritual knowledge is that in which the individual bases personal beliefs on personal experiences. In the past, religious knowledge has been predominant, and many subscribed to the "faith of their fathers" unquestionably. In the Aquarian Age, the primary moving force will be spiritual knowledge. The rising interest in such schools of thought as yoga, Wicca, the original Qabbalistic Judaism, and the Native American and African nature religions, which encourage spiritual experience rather than enforce religious dogma, illustrates that shift in awareness.

Another change will be the way in which one seeks spiritual experience. In the Piscean Age, the way to transcend the temptations and attachments of the material world and seek spiritual revelation was to retire to a monastery or ashram and embrace a life of near-solitary meditation and scriptural study. Many reached enlightenment this way, and the world is better for it, but this is not the Aquarian way. The deity of the Aquarian Age is the Divine Spark that exists in the minds and hearts of all human beings, and nothing reinforces belief in this Divine Spark more than being out among people, training oneself to see God in each of them.

One of the most popular spiritual leaders of our century was Swami Muktananda, who represents a near-perfect transitional figure. Muktananda reached enlightenment himself through retreat; he lived in a hut under a mango tree for twelve years until he attained self-realization. When he himself embraced the life of a guru, he attracted thousands of followers from all over the world who came to his ashram at Ganeshpuri, India. His devotees wanted to stay there for the rest of their lives, learning at the feet of the Master. Muktananda eventually kicked most of them out, telling them that they had spent enough time away from the world and it was time for them to take their knowledge home. "Living in the world," he would say, "is the best possible *sadhana* there is."

This kind of spiritual pursuit will be most popular in the

Aquarian Age: to avoid becoming enmeshed in the physical world while living in the midst of all its potential snares. Though spiritually inclined people will continue to have material possessions, personal relationships, and power, they will be able to involve themselves with these matters without becoming dependent on them. (The Buddha taught that a person could become just as attached to poverty as to luxury.) The true saint is equally comfortable in both poverty and opulence, and part of the spirit of the Aquarian Age will be to attain material equality for all.

Preparing Yourself for the Aquarian Age

This is the kind of world in which we will live our future lives: a world where it is acknowledged, on spiritual, scientific, and social levels, that all are one, and yet the individual is still important. Not all of us are ready for such a world. Years ago, when I first began actively exploring the concept of a new age, I attended a lecture given by San Francisco, California, psychic Jeanne Borgen, who put it this way: "Earth is changing from a third to a fourth-dimensional vibration. Those who are not prepared for a fourth-dimensional life will be leaving; those who are will stay, but it will be an entirely different world."

Jeanne Borgen's words, spoken in 1975, seem strangely prophetic. It was only a few years before that astronomers became aware of black holes, quasars, neutron stars, and other cosmic enigmas. Some visionary astronomers have proposed that quasars, black holes, and possibly the more recently discovered white holes represent gateways between the dimensions. Is it too far-fetched to speculate that these strange astronomical phenomena could only become visible to Earth astronomers when Earth herself began to change her dimensional vibration?

A fourth-dimensional planet would be an incredible world indeed. A world where science and mysticism meet, where space travel and possibly time and inter-dimensional travel are commonplace might seem like science fiction to us. A world where the differences between individuals are perceived as illusory, as part of the Dance of Shiva, as part of a Divine game, might seem like something out of a mystic's book of visions, but we must remember to view the new concepts from a framework of active intelligence rather than of ignorance and mystery.

What exactly is involved in the process of Earth's changing from a third to a fourth dimension—and what did Jeanne Borgen mean when she said that "those not ready for a fourth-dimensional world will be leaving"? In recent decades there have been on the market many books which take the viewpoint that there is going to be some kind of cataclysm, some gigantic holocaust that will wipe out most of the population of the Earth. Some believe that it will be the Armageddon described in the Book of Revelation; others expect earthquakes, nuclear war, or the reappearance of Atlantis to destroy much of life on Earth as we know it.

Though worldwide disaster is a possibility, I do not believe that the necessary change of consciousness can only be accomplished by a full-fledged purging. Perhaps third-dimensional types will simply live out their lifespans and then leave, taking future incarnations on a third-dimensional planet other than Earth. Many children being born now seem exceptional: highly intelligent and (for those who have reached an age when they can understand) very open to "new age" consciousness. It is as if they have come into incarnation already prepared for a fourth-dimensional life.

How can you judge if you are ready for a fourth-dimensional life? Do not be too quick to assume that you are "Aquarian" simply because you are interested in new age thought. Are you ready to embrace a more simple lifestyle—voluntarily?

Are you genuinely prepared to "love your neighbor as yourself" and to "judge not, that you be not judged"? Are you capable of seeing God in everyone? We don't know—and cannot know—where we are on the curve of enlightenment. Nor can we judge anyone else's spiritual state.

How can we prepare ourselves for a series of lifetimes in the enlightened Age of Aquarius and in the Age of Capricorn which will inevitably follow, giving structure to all the knowledge and ideals acquired in the Aquarian Age?

First of all, you may ask, why make the effort? If we are not already prepared for a fourth-dimensional life, why bother to prepare for it? Why not just reincarnate on Alpha Centauri V or whatever third-dimensional planet our guides have in mind for us?

One reason might be this planet's great beauty. I have been working in the field of past-life regression for twelve years, and I have guided many people through previous lifetimes on other planets. I have yet to regress anyone who found him-or herself on a world that surpassed the rich diversity of colors, climates, and life forms which appear on Earth. Few planets can boast of the trees, the flowers, the insects, butterflies, birds, and mammals that make our planet the wonderful world it is. One of my clients called Earth "the most beautiful planet in the known Universe."

Second, this planet is our home. We have lived on Earth many hundreds or even thousands of lifetimes; our imprint and that of our ancestors is on this world, whether in ancient Sumer, India, Egypt, Rome, medieval Europe, or the South Sea Islands. We have left pieces of ourselves in every corner of this world. Whether we are most drawn to Greek sculpture, to Italian painting, or to Japanese flower arranging, the traces of our development as beings are here and there is every reason to want to continue to add to our heritage until it is time for us to move on to the next plane.

Third, the human race has never balked at challenges.

Human beings have always pushed on to explore new territories, new fields of knowledge, new inventions. Isn't a new age the most interesting challenge there could be? It might make us feel more secure to move sideways and take future incarnations on a comfortably third-dimensional planet, but is this really in keeping with the nature of the human race? My feeling is that it is not. For this reason I feel that anyone, whether you consider yourself "Piscean" or "Aquarian," aware enough to be reading this book can move on to the next section and begin to prepare for the new age.

Self-Help, the "Me Generation," and Change

In the 1970s a movement was launched that conservative psychologists and sociologists comtemptuously referred to as the "Me generation." The movement comprised many programs for self-improvement and consequent enhancement of our lives. People began wondering about and exploring their own potential for personal growth through psycho-technologies such as Transcendental Meditation, est, and Silva Mind Control. In doing so, they grew more independent, confident and understanding, and more aware of the world around them.

The cynicism surrounding the "Me generation" is, in my opinion, misplaced. Though some people took up these practices strictly for selfish reasons, and some psycho-technology gurus got rich quick, a significant number of people approached self-improvement with a different attitude: "How can I understand others if I don't understand me?"

This question is a significant truth that must be faced before anyone can really approach making a difference in the world. It is very difficult to change the world; it is much easier to change yourself. Part of the change in social consciousness is not so much the result of political activism (although that is part of it) as it is of people coming to terms with themselves and attaining a degree of inner peace. For it is much easier to see how others are making themselves unhappy—and to be aware of ways in which they can help themselves—if you have already attained a degree of happiness within yourself.

A new age bumper sticker reads, "Let there be Peace on Earth—and Let it Begin With Me." I am a strong proponent of this philosophy, and I believe absolutely in its effectiveness. It is not only desirable, it is vital to our survival on this planet that we find inner peace. For if a million people attain peace within themselves, how can they make war on each other? War, crime, poverty, and cutthroat politics and business practices are all the result of unhappiness and discontent. They represent desperate attempts on the parts of the individuals involved to find happiness in something outside themselves. But this never works. Power, money, material possessions, and fame may give you a moment's satisfaction, but in the long run the inner discontent will surface again, and spark still another desperate search for something outside.

The Role of Self-Improvement

Whatever self improvements you have already pursued, or are planning to work on, will no doubt enrich your present life, and the advances you make are going to enrich your future lives as well. This works on two levels. First of all, by finding a sense of inner peace within yourself now, you and everyone else who is doing the same are creating an energy that will spread and that will eventually help to alter the consciousness of society as a whole. Consequently, your future lives may be lived in a world where everyone is at peace and where life is a constant challenge—not to survive, but to learn more and to seek new horizons for ourselves and our descendants.

Second, self-improvement now—doing away with all the phobias and hangups that plague you lifetime after lifetime—clears your psyche so that you will go into your future incarnations with a cleaner slate. You have less karma to bog you down, and therefore you are freer to move on and seek happiness on all levels, doing what you do best. You are also freer to seek knowledge of and unity with the Divine, to get closer to the ultimate transformation: enlightenment.

How Astrology Can Help

In recent years, the ancient science of astrology has turned away from being a fatalistic tool for fortune tellers and become valuable in psychological evaluation. Since the mid-1970s—the first major blossoming of the "Me generation"—many people with an interest in self-improvement have turned to astrology for guidance. Psychologists such as Zipporah Dobyns, Liz Greene, and Howard Sasportas have used astrology to enhance their psychology practices and found it most enlightening. Many of my own clients who have been in psychotherapy for years have said in amazement: "You told me in an hour what it took my therapist a year to find out!" Astrology can be a valuable aid in psychotherapy and self-actualization. The key lies in studying the most positive manifestation of the astrological factors in your chart and accentuating them in your life. For a complete understanding of this method, you need to have your astrological chart cast and read by a professional astrologer. For those who have not yet had a chance to do this, the following paragraphs may provide a good beginning.

For those of you who are familiar with astrology and have had your charts done, I want to emphasize that I do not exclusively use Sun signs to interpret personality. I use the

Sun signs here as a guideline for beginners in the field. If you are familiar with your chart and are aware of influences other than your Sun sign that have a strong effect on your character, be sure to consider them as well. For instance, if your Sun is in Aries and your Moon is in Cancer you will want to consider the Cancer section as well as Aries. The following paragraphs give a basic sketch of the characteristics of each sign and what things should be developed in order to prepare the individual for present and future lives in the Age of Aquarius. Accompanying each paragraph is an affirmation for each sign, to use in meditation or as a written affirmation, which can help you to develop the highest and most Aquarian attributes of the sign.

Aries

March 20—April 20
Cardinal Fire
Ruler: Mars

Affirmation: "Vigilant but unafraid, I forge ahead."

Aries is the "I Am" sign of the zodiac, and represents the newly born. Therefore, some Ariens tend to have childish behavior patterns: stubborness, impulsiveness, impatience, and so on. Like young children making their first forays from the safety of the home into the world, Ariens often charge blindly and enthusiastically ahead, heedless of danger. The Ariens are the pioneers of the zodiac, the first to embrace new concepts and new ideas, and their enthusiasms can appear to be boundless, ever seeking higher mountains to ascend. For this reason, highly evolved Ariens are probably the most susceptible to new age thought and the most eager to try new ideas and practices.

From the Aquarian point of view, Ariens might be considered "spiritual scientists," seeking the right combination of higher technology and its relationships with the spiritual realm. And if Ariens do not find the proper combination, they simply try another one, and continue to search until it is found. The indomitability and the pioneering spirit of Ariens serve them well in the Aquarian Age, and therefore these are the traits that Ariens should work on developing to their highest possible manifestation. The above affirmation can help Ariens to develop these traits and to pull themselves out of the occasional lows life can sometimes inflict.

The impulsiveness that makes Ariens want to explore also can make them blind to the presence of danger—to themselves and to others. While developing the traits of leadership, exploration, and conquest, the Arien needs also to make special efforts to be aware of possible perils and to take precautions to guard against them. The Aquarian Age, will involve concentration in fields such as artificial intelligence, mental technology, aerospace, science, space exploration, and planetary engineering, all of which involve conditions and elements of the unknown, dangerous or otherwise. The Arien needs to develop caution without compromising curiosity or adventureousness. For this reason the affirmation above includes the word, "vigilant."

Ariens' biggest problem usually involves relationships with other people. In the zodiac, Aries opposes Libra, and the two signs are called the Aries-Libra axis. The Aries-Libra axis is primarily concerned with the problem of self (Aries) versus society (Libra). Complete immersion in self (Aries) implies complete rejection of and by society (Libra). Complete freedom (Aries) indicates a total absence of relationships (Libra). Many of you reading this were probably born when Saturn, Neptune, and/or Pluto was in Libra; therefore, if Aries is strong in your chart you may have karmic obligations remaining from prior lives to learn more about dealing with society and other people in general. Unless other factors in the chart offset the sign's egocentrism, Aries people tend to see others as extensions of themselves rather than individuals in their own right. They often are shocked when the desires of those they love don't entirely mesh with their own. This can be and often is the result of past lives as loners, with few if any relationships. If you are an Aries, you need to work through this "I Am" tendency in order to make your relationships, both in the present and in future lives, become a source of joy rather than strain.

Taurus

April 21—May 21
Fixed Earth
Ruler: Venus

Affirmation: "I am the Earth; the Earth am I. From within me grows the future."

Taurus is the first of the earth signs, and Taureans are often said to have "green thumbs." They are among the best gardeners in the zodiac, having not only the patience to see a garden through from seed to harvest, but a sense of identification with the Earth that enables them to make the plants grow faster and healthier. Their inner passions make them the master ecologists of the zodiac, who dream of creating the purest of earthly environments. The love and warmth inherent in the Taurean nature will make Taureans highly instrumental in spreading the sense of the oneness of humanity that will mark the Aquarian Age.

The problems Taureans have in the new Age will probably be rooted in their innate stodginess and the desire to conserve energy. Taureans may be unwilling to make an effort to change things—or themselves. For this reason, Taureans seeking enlightenment need to concentrate on producing a result.

Taurus's opposite sign is Scorpio, and the Taurus-Scorpio axis is related to values. Everything that humanity has been taught to value—love, money, power, sex, material possessions—is ruled by Taurus or Scorpio. As many of you Taureans reading this were also born with either Saturn, Uranus, or Neptune in Scorpio, you probably have obligation remaining from past lives to reassess your value systems. A Taurus probably has placed too much emphasis on power, money, love, and the other things of the world in past lives, and therefore in the current life needs to emphasize using Taurean generosity to put these qualities to work for self and others. Taureans may do this best through artistic or charitable pursuits.

If the sense of identification with the Earth is developed to the highest degree, the Taurean can enter the Aquarian Age with the necessary knowledge, motivation, productivity, and spiritual awareness to contribute immensely to the well-being of all creatures on Earth. The affirmation above is designed to invoke the innate sense of identification with the Earth that dwells within all Taureans and to bring it to awareness.

Gemini

May 22—June 21
Mutable Air
Ruler: Mercury

Affirmation: "Unite me with myself, bring my mind to my heart; let me see beyond my intellect into the realm of the Aquarian spirit.

Gemini is ruled by Mercury, which is the quickest planet in the solar system, and hence Gemini is associated with quickness, both of body and of mind. Gemini, more than any other sign of the zodiac, represents pure intellect, and therefore Geminis are often among the most mentally-oriented of Earth beings.

The drawback is that Geminis often seek intellectual answers to emotional and spiritual questions. They also have a hard time experiencing and expressing feelings. Queen Victoria, a triple Gemini—Sun, Moon, Ascendant—was often accused of being cold and unfeeling. Strictly speaking, Geminians like Victoria are not cold; they simply have little concept of feelings beyond their own. In other words, empathy is not their strong suit. The tendency of the Gemini to change roles frequently, to make 180-degree changes in viewpoint, and to abandon projects long before they are complete, can drive their friends and families crazy.

What Geminis need to know is that the two sides of their mercurial nature don't have to be contradictory; the two opposing points of view can be balanced and brought together to form a cohesive whole, resulting in completion of commitments and projects. Geminians need to use their intellect to develop a true understanding of matters of the heart, and to make a special effort to cultivate that side of their natures. Past-life research shows that when the feelings are repressed in one life, they can come back like high tide in the next, producing an overabundance of emotion that can become uncontrollable. Therefore, if you are a Gemini who tries to apply logic to your feelings, you could benefit from attempting to experience your emotions rather than repressing them. In this way, you will be working towards an equitable balance between intellect and emotion in your future lives.

There is no doubt that Geminian intellect will be a big plus in the Aquarian Age. However, the innate lack of empathy and lack of commitment in this sign can seriously limit the effectiveness of the Gemini. For this reason, the affirmation above is designed to enable Geminians to bring head and heart together and to unite the two different sides of their natures, forming a whole human being.

Cancer

June 22—July 23
Cardinal Water
Ruler: The Moon

Affirmation: "I love you—I set you free—and so allow myself to be me."

As pointed out earlier in this chapter, the Aquarian Age will be marked by a sense of unity throughout the world. For this reason the loving, nurturing nature of Cancer will be vitally needed.

Cancers, male and female, tend to manifest the nurturing usually associated with motherhood, sometimes to a fault. This sign is associated with home, mother, and family, and many Cancers are quite attached to their homes and surroundings. They are also very traditional in their viewpoints. The main drawback of this type of attachment is the tendency to cling to what should be let go. This includes children, lovers, places, attitudes, and customs.

Unlike Geminis, Cancers are naturally warm, sympathetic, and sensitive to the feelings of others. When Cancer people see anyone in physical or emotional pain, they identify with that pain and try to help relieve it. This tendency can be carried to extremes, however, and Cancer's over-protectiveness sometimes causes stress to those they are trying to help. One of the most difficult lessons for the Cancer individual to learn is to let go, to open the crab's claws and let loved ones venture out on their own. Once this lesson is mastered, Cancers will find that through releasing their loved ones they have released themselves as well, for when they stop identifying with those they love, they can meet new people whom they will probably like very much: themselves.

Cancer people need to learn to detach themselves from the intense feelings associated with this sign and be more objective when assessing their lives, particularly during times of change. As stated in the affirmation above, perhaps the most difficult lesson for Cancers to learn is loving enough to let go.

Leo

July 24—August 23
Fixed Fire
Ruler: The Sun

Affirmation: "Release me from my ego; allow me to love without fear of rejection. Grant me the ability to see from the reflected viewpoint of my fellow beings."

The symbol for Leo is the lion, king of beasts, ferocious and unyielding, secure in his rulership and yet loving, generous, and capable of bestowing largesse upon all around him. Leos are known for being regal, for taking center stage. They are performers, capable of giving impressive performances, and yet totally sincere in their love and loyalty. They are proud, sometimes egotistical, determined to do the best for their little circle. However, too often the lion does not have the awareness to see beyond his or her pride and to realize that there are other beings who need generosity as well. Leos are talented, good-hearted, and charismatic, but if they are to fit into an Aquarian society, they must transcend their egos and identify with the feelings of others, even those whom they may never meet. There is nothing wrong with having a healthy ego; it is often necessary if you are going to make a mark in the world. Nonetheless, the best rulers have always been those who were most involved with the lives and hearts of their people.

Since each sign implies its opposite, deep within the Leo is the Aquarian capacity to identify with the masses, with the unseen faces that represent our fellow human beings. Too much Leo self-centeredness in one lifetime can lead to being in need of Aquarian charity in the next. Therefore, in order to avoid this future-life trap, Leos need to work towards sublimating their self-centeredness and developing the latent Aquarian side of their nature.

The affirmation above is formulated to allow the Leo to transcend attachment to the ego, not to annihilate it, as some Eastern philosophies recommend. In doing this, Leos will enable themselves to use their royal abilities in order to reach out and assist the people of the Aquarian Age without giving up the innate power, strength, charisma, generosity, and loving nature of the mighty lion.

Virgo

August 24—September 23
Mutable Earth
Ruler: Mercury

Affirmation: "Let me serve myself through my service to humanity, accepting the credit for my own magnificence."

Virgos are the servants of humanity. Virgos will accept and perform the most menial of tasks, often without complaint. They make conscientious, loyal, efficient, and practical employees, and their eye for detail renders them excellent in careers that require meticulousness and accuracy. In the Age of Aquarius, the Virgoan virtues will be greatly needed in order to keep the idealistic, intellectual Aquarian society in tune with the practical concerns of life. Virgos might become the foundations and cornerstones of the new social structure, and the managers of Aquarian concepts, bringing Aquarian ideals down to Earth.

Virgos in Aquarian society, however, may tend to keep their noses to the grindstone too much, to get lost in detail, to lose sight of the entire picture and long-term goals. They are usually their own worst critics and may turn that criticism on others around them—which can be highly irritating to the Aquarian!

Virgo is the "I Analyze" sign of the zodiac. Too often, Virgoans, in an endless quest for perfection, can turn their obsession with minute matters and analysis against both themselves and those around them, creating an image of pickiness that can undermine their own self-esteem and the self-images of those they love. Too much Virgoan analysis in one life can lead to a total absence of Piscean vision in the next. (Pisces, the visionary sign of the zodiac, is the polar opposite of Virgo.) Therefore, Virgoans need to learn to curb their innate pickiness and look beyond it, attempting to see the whole instead of simply the sum of the parts.

The affirmation outlined above will enable Virgos to use their penchant for detail as a tool to finely hone and perfect any task they undertake in order to contribute to Aquarian society.

Libra

September 24—October 23
Cardinal Air
Ruler: Venus

Affirmation: "Let the balance of my inner being reach forth into the world, giving myself and humanity a proper balance between the physical, mental, and spiritual worlds."

The symbol for Libra is the scales, and indeed the focus of the lives of Librans appears to be a constant search for balance. Libra is associated with marriage, balancing the energies between male and female; with business, balancing supply and demand; and with education, balancing different fields of knowledge. Libra is also connected with law and justice; one of the common images associated with Libra is the figure of the Goddess Themis, blindfolded, holding the scales of justice in her right hand. To this end, the skills of the Libran in the Aquarian Age can manifest themselves as bringing forth the law of God and humanity in its purest spiritual form. Librans of the Aquarian Age might be the enlightened magistrates who apply not the arbitrary laws of people, too often tailored to the limited needs of special-interest groups, but the highest laws applicable to an advanced society.

Unfortunately, Librans have a tendency to immerse themselves too much in social convention. You will recall what we said about the Aries-Libra axis. While Aries tends to become too involved in self and what the individual wants, Libra swings too far in the other direction. Librans—particularly those who, like many of you reading this, were born with Neptune in Libra—tend to ignore what they need as individuals in favor of doing "what's right," what is socially acceptable, or what their partners want. Complete immersion in society (Libra) tends to lead to a complete absence (or confusion) about one's self-image (Aries). Complete subjugation to relationships (Libra) implies a total absence of freedom (Aries).

While on the surface this may seem unselfish and admirable, in the long run such complete self-sacrifice can cause pent-up resentment and hurt your relationships. If you are a Libran, you need to work through this tendency to place your own needs second to those of others and learn to express your own needs more. In this way, your self-image, both in this life and in future lives, will be strengthened, and you will be more confident in your ability to help society in the Aquarian Age.

The Libran need to balance too often manifests as an unwillingness to take a stand, because the Libran always sees both sides of any question. This weakness will be inappropriate in the new Age; one of the most frustrating traits associated with Aquarius—and hence with the Age that bears its name—is intellectual stubbornness. The Libran will have to weigh the scales of justice and then be firm. The affirmation above is designed to enable the Libran not only to see both sides clearly, but to apply the laws to each particular situation and achieve absolute fairness to both sides.

Scorpio

October 24—November 22
Fixed Water
Ruler: Pluto

Affirmation: "Release me from the lower limits of my ego and bring forth from within me the Phoenix energy of rebirth."

The transformative energies of Scorpio will be vital in the Age of Aquarius. The principle inherent in Scorpio is "transform or die," and many people who are too attached to Piscean ways will have to do just that. It is for this reason that the Scorpion, whose life is a continuous series of transformations, will be among the leaders of the Aquarian Age, helping people through the continuous process of being reborn again and again (all in one lifetime!).

With Scorpio, there appears to be no halfway point. In fact, the phrase "The greatest of sinners, the greatest of saints" often has been applied to Scorpio. Scorpios have an innate sense of unity with the underlying forces of the Universe. Hence they will be leaders in the Aquarian Age, contributing to the inner transformation of each individual and the resulting psychological well-being of society. Scorpios will be first to realize an understanding of the hidden atomic forces necessary for Aquarian technology to master before advanced science can be united with ancient metaphysical knowledge.

Scorpio, like its polar opposite Taurus, is related to values, particularly with regard to power. Too often Scorpios are tempted to use power simply for its own sake. For example, Scorpio is associated with sex, and Scorpios frequently are called the "sexiest" members of the zodiac. However, some astrologers have observed that Scorpios often do not value sex for its own sake, but for the power it gives them over their partners. Money often serves the same purpose. Many Scorpios, gifted with an ability to create money, will accumulate piles of it simply for the power it brings. Power can be used to create a better world, but it can also corrupt. Scorpios need to learn to channel their power not for ego gratification but to better themselves and the world around them.

Scorpios are secretive and tend to repress their knowledge, selfishly keeping transformational awareness to themselves. In the Aquarian Age, this won't work, as the Aquarian Water-bearer's role is to pour the water of wisdom over all the world. The affirmation for Scorpio is designed to enable these people to let the power of their inner knowledge be shared with all.

Sagittarius

November 23—December 21
Mutable Fire
Ruler: Jupiter

Affirmation: "Allow me to seek the knowledge of the new Age and to bring it forth into the light with integrity, love, and wisdom."

The key word for Sagittarius is *expansion*, and Sagittarians are indeed expansive in their ways. They are outgoing, talkative, and charming—the life of the party. However, Sagittarians are moralists who operate almost entirely from ideals, believing (at least in the first part of life) in the ultimate goodness of human nature. This rather unrealistic viewpoint can lead to bitter disillusionment later in life, when these people discover that those whom they set on pedestals have feet of clay like everyone else. As a result, Sagittarians may find themselves approaching new relationships and new situations, which they formerly welcomed enthusiastically as exciting new experiences, with distrust. Past-life research shows that when someone learns to distrust people and to expect betrayal (as disillusioned Sagittarians too often do) he or she tends to attract the sort of person who fills that image—and this tendency may spill over into future lives. Therefore, the Sagittarian needs to cultivate a more realistic view of the world and the people in it.

In the Aquarian Age, teachers with the expressive abilities of Sagittarius will be invaluable, for new knowledge on all levels will be appearing on the horizon every day, and it will take the expansive and talkative Sagittarian to spread the word effectively. However, the Sagittarian's effectiveness as a teacher is somewhat limited by a desire to keep on spreading knowledge, even when the teacher has emptied his or her store of knowledge completely. Some Sagittarians will expound sagely about things of which they know nothing. Sagittarians need to take time to listen to others, so they can replenish themselves. In this way, they can use their talents to make effective contributions to Aquarian society.

Capricorn

December 22—January 21
Cardinal Earth
Ruler: Saturn

Affirmation: "Allow me to bring forth the warmth hidden within me and to use it with love and caring to give structure to the ideals all around me."

The planetary ruler of Capricorn is Saturn, and Saturn bestows form and structure to matters ruled by all the other planets. Hence Capricorn is associated with ambition, business, caution, and organizational abilities, as well as with traditional values and conservative attitudes. These traits, looking towards the future Age of Capricorn (which follows the Age of Aquarius) will be vital to the Aquarian Age; Capricorn abilities will help give structure, form, and practical application to the high-flown ideals and concepts of Aquarian society. Capricorns also will keep the fast-moving people of the Aquarian Age in touch with their past and its traditions, and help prevent them from throwing themselves too enthusiastically into ungrounded and unproven social structures and concepts.

Capricorns have too often been branded as cold, unfeeling, and rigid in their attitudes, and for many pure types these traits may hold true. However, Capricorn is an earth sign, and, buried deep though it may be, the same earthiness associated with Taurus and Virgo exists, and if tapped may be put to good use. Therefore Capricorns need to exercise this capability to transcend their rigidness and conservatism and expand their horizons. Past-life research reveals that those who are too rigid in their outlook in one life may find themselves in the next incarnation the victims of reactionary views held by others. For this reason, Capricorns need to learn to look beyond tradition and use it to provide a foundation for future growth.

Not unlike the Missouri mule, Capricorns are "cursed" with a basic failure to yield to or to believe in anything that they cannot see, hear, feel, or taste. Visions and metaphysical concepts, because they are not tangible, can be extremely difficult for these people to grasp. Capricorns need to learn to warm up and open their hearts to matters beyond the physical, and to learn to apply them just as they apply principles of business practice. The above affirmation is formulated especially for that purpose.

Aquarius

January 22—February 20
Fixed Air
Ruler: Uranus

Affirmation: "Allow me to spread the waters of the new Age to every individual, giving each human being what he or she deserves, including myself."

Welcome to your own era, Aquarius! This is the time when Aquarian virtues will blossom, when the high ideals, devotion to knowledge, and love of the masses associated with this sign will come forth and be utilized to the highest degree. You will be an ecstatic witness to the marriage of science and metaphysics, to the unity of the Universal Church with the ideal state. The expansion of humanity's horizons to other planets, other dimensions, and perhaps even other times is something the Aquarian has been looking forward to since the dawn of the Age of Reason, and it will not be long until those goals are reached. Aquarians, needless to say, will be at the forefront of all this expansive activity.

All this will happen only if Aquarians allow themselves to relax their fixed-sign stubbornness long enough to listen to the ideas of others. For Aquarians, aware of and comfortable with their own intellectual abilities, often fail to give others the credit they deserve, and too often get so attached in their own concepts that they hinder their own progress. The spirit of the Aquarian Age is cooperation. While Aquarius has long been associated with that virtue, there are times when obstinacy comes into conflict with that basic Aquarian drive.

The Aquarian falls short in the area of personal relationships. Unless other factors in the chart offset this tendency, Aquarians tend to focus their love-energies less on the people immediately surrounding them and more on the unknown poor and needy. Many radical politicians and social workers are Aquarians; they often make a big difference to the people they serve. Yet these same people may neglect their families and close friends, appearing to be somewhat cold and distant. My research into past lives reveals that an overabundance of Aquarian impersonal love in one lifetime can lead, in future lives, to a desperate need for close personal relationships in an environment when no one is there. Aquarians need to extend their sense of solidarity beyond the faceless masses and into their immediate circle, and particularly to themselves, for we feel most generous with knowledge and other gifts when we ourselves are secure in our own possession of them. Aquarians have long been known for their willingness to pour the waters of benevolence over all the peoples of the world, but they need to learn to save a little for themselves.

Pisces

February 20—March 19
Mutable Water
Ruler: Neptune

Affirmation: "Release me from the ancient limitations of the previous Age and allow me to go forth into the coming Age with warmth, sensitivity, compassion, and foresight."

Though the Age of Pisces is ending, the positive virtues of Pisces—as best exemplified by Jesus Christ—will be much more necessary and much more pronounced in the Age of Aquarius. For although the overall aura of the Aquarian Age will be higher thought and expansion into higher realms, if the intellectualism of Aquarius is allowed to go unchecked by Piscean love, compassion, warmth, sensitivity, and mysticism, the Aquarian Age would eventually become too scientific and too intellectualized. Aquarius is an air sign, and air signs focus on intellect rather than on feeling. The gifts of Pisces will be needed in the Aquarian Age. For this reason the Piscean needs to concentrate on developing them to their highest potential, pressing past the innate fear, reclusiveness, and tendency toward procrastination that are the less desirable traits associated with the sign.

The keyword for Pisces and its planetary ruler, Neptune, is escape. Those under the influence of Neptune or Pisces passionately desire expanded consciousness and want to escape from the mundane affairs of the world around them. And most of them do find the escape they crave. They can do it through positive pursuits such as art, music, poetry, or drama; or, on a more mystical level, through meditation and spiritual studies; or they might find their escape in darker ways—through workaholism, overeating, alcohol, tobacco, or drugs.

Pisceans need to learn to channel this basic need for escape into the more positive channels. On a broader level, they need to learn to balance their desire for escape with life on the material plane. In order to really escape this world, we need to learn to love it first, and that means savoring the blessings of this planet as well as trying to escape its darker side. My research indicates that those who retreat from the world due to a distaste for it are often hit with a multitude of worldly responsibilities and a sense of guilt and oppression in the next life. By achieving the proper balance this trap can be circumvented, and your future lives will be experiences to treasure.

The above affirmation is, of course, designed for that purpose—and so, good luck, Pisces, as you move into your future lives!

Using the Affirmations

Of the above affirmations, your Sun sign not withstanding, seek out the one(s) that stirs within you the strongest feelings. Use this as either a written affirmation or a meditation.

Written Affirmations

After you have chosen the affirmation best suited to you, take a piece of paper and a pen, a typewriter, or a word processor, and simply write the affirmation again and again. Repeat the words as you write them. In doing this, you are thinking, hearing, saying, seeing, and writing the affirmation; hence you are creating a mental overload that will impress the sentiments deeply into your mind. Even if you watch TV or listen to music while doing this, the message will continue to drum itself into your subconscious as you continue to write it.

Then take one page of the written message and tape it to your bathroom mirror. Take another and fasten it to the wall above your desk. Take as many pages as you want and pin them wherever you feel you will have the most exposure to them. Even when you reach the point where you no longer consciously notice that the pages are there, you will still be absorbing them into your psyche, and eventually you will find that you are living the message.

Meditation

Sit or lie in a comfortable place, away from noise or distractions, preferably alone, but, if you desire, with other meditators. Close your eyes and allow whatever goes on within your mind to be there, and then concentrate on repeating the affirmation to yourself in a singsong manner, creating a rhythm synchronized with your breathing. Eventually you may reach a point where you are in such a deep state of meditation that you no longer feel the need to repeat the affirmation aloud, but the message still will appear in your mind's eye. If you continue this practice every day, or as often as you possibly can, you eventually will find that you are living the message, and you will have taken a major step toward achieving your goal of becoming an aware citizen of the Age of Aquarius.

Notes

1. Robert Hand, "The Age and Constellation of Pisces," *Essays on Astrology* (West Chester, PA: Whitford Press, 1982) pp. 147-148.
2. Edouard Schure, *The Great Initiates* (New York: Harper & Row, Publishers, 1961), chapter 23.
3. Hand, p. 152.
4. Fritjof Capra, *The Tao of Physics* (Boulder, CO: Shambhala, 1975), p. 44.
5. Edgar Mitchell, from lecture given at the Whole Life Expo, Los Angeles, CA, October 1987.

ABOUT THE AUTHORS

Kelynda has been interested in metaphysics for most of her life. She is accomplished in many areas, including psychic development, Tarot, astrology, dream work, and crystals, and teaches and lectures on these subjects. She is also the author of *The Crystal Tree,* (Whitford Press), and is currently working on a book *The Magnificent Quest,* which expands upon the concepts she introduces herein.

Edward Sparks has been a student and practitioner of metaphysics and nutrition for twenty-five years. He conducts workshops, seminars and lectures nationwide on such diverse subjects as past-life regression and firewalking. Currently he is writing a vegetarian cookbook and a book entitled *There Are No Incurable Diseases.*

Brad Steiger has been a researcher, lecturer, counselor and teacher of metaphysical subjects for more than thirty years, and he is one of the leading figures in the New Age movement. He is the author of over one hundred books, thousands of articles, and conducts workshops and lectures internationally.

Enid Hoffman is a respected lecturer and teacher in psychic development and Huna, and speaks on these subjects internationally. She is also the author of *Develop Your Psychic Skills, Expand Your Psychic Skills, Huna: A Beginner's Guide,* and *Hands: A Complete Guide to Palmistry,* (Whitford Press).

Nicki Scully is a teacher and lecturer, specializing in Egyptian Huna, and has traveled throughout North and South America spreading her knowledge. She has also produced a tape entitled "The Cauldron of Thoth" which contains some of her teachings. Several of her other "journeys" will be available on casette tapes soon.

Mary Devlin is a certified astrologer with expertise in past-life work. She also is the author of two astrology books: *Astrology and Past Lives* and *Astrology and Relationships,* (Whitford Press). She maintains an active astrological practice in California and is currently working with Edward Sparks on a vegetarian cookbook.